Planet
Earth

PRINCETON ▪ LONDON

Published in the United States and Canada by
Two-Can Publishing LLC
234 Nassau Street
Princeton, NJ 08542

www.two-canpublishing.com

'Two-Can' is a trademark of Two-Can Publishing
Two-Can Publishing is a division of Zenith Entertainment plc,
43–45 Dorset Street, London W1H 4AB

Hardback ISBN 1-58728-0493
Hardback 1 2 3 4 5 6 7 8 9 10 02 01 00

COVER

Cover designed by Picthall and Gunzi Ltd. Photographs courtesy of
Space Frontiers Ltd (Earth), Telegraph Colour Library; Dominic
Zwemmer (rock carvings/Namibia); A.C. Twomey (avalanche/Mount
Everest) and Simon Fraser (wild garlic), Science Photo Library

MOUNTAINS

Author: Catherine Bradley; Consultant: Roger Hammond, Director of
Living Earth, UK; Story by Claire Watts; Editor: Monica Byles; US
Editor: Karen Ingebretsen, World Book Publishing; Designer: Belinda
Webster. Photographs: p.6-7 Bruce Coleman/Dieter & Mary Plage;
p.9 (top) Bruce Coleman/Steve Kaufman, (bottom) Bruce
Coleman/C.B. & D.W. Frith; p.10 (left) Zefa/Ned Gillette, (center)
London/Ian Beames; p.11 (right) Bruce Coleman/Stephen J.
Krasemann; p.12 (bottom left) Ardea, London/François Gohier, (top
right) Ardea, London/Kenneth W. Fink, (right) Bruce Coleman/Hans
Reinhard, (bottom right) Survival Anglia/Clive Huggins; p.14 Survival
Anglia/Jeff Foott; p.15 (top) Bruce Coleman/Erwin and Peggy Bauer,
(bottom) Bruce Coleman/Steve Kaufman; p.16 Bruce Coleman/C.B.
& D.W. Frith; p.17 (top) Survival Anglia/Richard & Julia Kemp,
(bottom left) Ardea, London/Eric Dragesco, (bottom) Ardea,
London/Kenneth W. Fink; p.18 (top) Hutchison Library; p.19
Ardea, London/Richard Waller; p.20 (bottom left) Ardea, London/
S. Roberts, (right) Hutchison Library/Zefa; p.22 Bruce Coleman/Hans
Reinhard; p.23 Bruce Coleman/Dieter & Mary Plage; p.24 Bruce
Coleman/Gerald Cubitt; p.24 Bruce Coleman/M.P. Price.
Illustrations by Michaela Stewart.

DESERTS

Author & Designer: Lucy Baker; Consultant: Roger Hammond,
Director of Living Earth, UK. Photographs: p.34 (left) Heather
Angel/Biofotos, (right) NHPA; p.35 Biofotos/Brian Rogers; p.37
Ardea/François Gohier; p.38 (left) Ardea/François Gohier, (right) Bruce
Coleman; p.39 Ardea; p.40 (top) Zefa/Klaus Hachenberg, (bottom) Bruce
Coleman/Carol Hughes; p.41 (top) Ardea/K.W. Fink, (bottom)
Ardea/François Gohier; p.42–43 Ardea/Clem Haagner; p.44 Planet
Earth/Hans Christian Heap; p.45 Science Photo Library/Keith Kent; p.46
(top) Ardea/Peter Steyn, (bottom) The Hutchison Library; p.47 Zefa/J.
Bitsch; p.48 (top) B.&C. Alexander, (bottom) Zefa/R. Steedman; p.49
Impact Photos/David Reed; p.50–51 Mark Edwards; p.52 Oxfam/Jeremy
Hartley; p.53 (top) Picturepoint, (bottom) Impact Photos/David Reed.
Illustrations by Francis Mosley. Story illustrated by Valerie McBride.

OCEANS

Author & Designer: Lucy Baker; Consultant: Roger Hammond, Director
of Living Earth, UK. Photographs: p.62 Greenpeace/Morgan; p.63
Ardea/François Gohier; p.65 Ardea/Ron & Valerie Taylor; p.66–67
Zefa/Dr D. James; p.68 Planet Earth/Robert Arnold; p.69 (top) Oxford
Scientific Films/Peter Parks, (bottom) Oxford Scientific Films/Peter
Parks; p.70 (top) Ardea/J-M Labat, (bottom) Oxford Scientific
Films/G.I. Bernard; p.71 (top left) Planet Earth/Peter David, (top right)
Planet Earth/Gillian Lythgoe, (bottom) Planet Earth/Peter Scoones;
p.72 Ardea/Ron & Valerie Taylor; p.73 Planet Earth/Peter David; p.74
Ardea/Clem Haagner; p.75 (top) Planet Earth/Jim Brandenburg,
(bottom) Ardea/François Gohier; p.76-77 B.&C. Alexander; p.78
Ardea/Richard Vaughan; p.79 Zefa; p.80-81 Ardea/François Gohier.
Illustrations by Francis Mosley. Artworking by Claire Legemah.

WOODLANDS

Author: Rosanne Hooper; Consultant: Keith Jones, Environmental
Consultant; Editor: Lucy Duke; US Editor: Karen Ingebretsen, World
Book Publishing; Designer: Fionna Robson. Photographs: p.90-91
Planet Earth/John Lythgoe; p.92 Bruce Coleman/Robert P. Carr; p.93
(top) Zefa/T. Martin, (bottom) Zefa/Robert Jureit; p.94 (top) Zefa,
(bottom) Frank Lane/M.J. Thomas; p.95 (top) Bruce Coleman/Jane
Burton, (bottom) Zefa; p.96 Planet Earth/Ken King; p.97 (right)
Zefa/G. Scott; p.98 Bruce Coleman/Scott Nielson; p.99 Bruce
Coleman/Hans Reinhard; p.100 Zefa/P.&T. Leeson; p.101 (top)
Planet Earth/William M. Smithey Jr., (bottom) Bruce Coleman/Joseph
Van Wormer; p.102 Zefa/E.&P. Bauer; p.103 (top) Bryan & Cherry
Alexander, (bottom) Biofotos/Heather Angel; p.104 Frank
Lane/E.&D. Hasking; p.105 (right) Image Bank/Grant Faint, (left)
Zefa; p.106-107 Bruce Coleman/Colin Molyneux; p.108 Still/Mark
Edwards; p.109 Panos/Penny Tweedie. Illustrations by Madeleine
David. Story illustrations by Ruth Rivers.

RAIN FORESTS

Author and designer: Lucy Baker; Consultant: Roger Hammond,
Director of Living Earth, UK. Photographs: p.119 Bruce Coleman;
p.121 (top) Heather Angel/Biofotos, (bottom) South American
Pictures/Tony Morrison; p.122 Bruce Coleman/E.&P. Bauer; p.123
Ardea/Pat Morris; p.124 (top) Ardea/Anthony & Elizabeth Bomford,
(bottom) Bruce Coleman/J. Mackinnon; p.125 (top) NHPA/L.H.
Newman, (center) Survival Anglia/Claude Steelman, (right) NHPA/Jany
Sauvanet; p.126 (bottom) Ardea, (top) Bruce Coleman; p.127 Bruce
Coleman; p.128 The Hutchison Library/J. Von Puttkamer; p.129 (top)
Survival International/Steve Cox, (bottom) The Hutchison Library/
J. Von Puttkamer; p.130 Bruce Coleman/Michael Fogden; p.131 Survival
International/Victor Englebert; p.132 Impact Photos; p.133 The
Hutchison Library; p.134–135 NHPA; p.136. Illustrations by Francis
Mosley. Story illustrated by Valerie McBride.

POLAR LANDS

Author & designer: Monica Byles. Consultant: Roger Hammond,
Director of Living Earth, UK. Edited by Claire Watts. Photograph
credits: p.146 (top) NHPA/Stephen Kraseman; p.146–147
NHPA/Gordon Claridge; p.149 Survival Anglia/Joel Bennett;
p.150 Ardea/Clem Haagner; p.152 (top) Survival Anglia/Rick Price,
(bottom) B.&C. Alexander; p.153 (top) Ardea, (bottom) Ardea/Jean-
Paul Ferrero; p.154 Ardea/E. Mickleburgh; p.155 (top) Ardea/Ron
& Valerie Taylor, (bottom) NHPA/Stephen Kraseman; p.156 Bruce
Coleman/Inigo Everson; p.157 (top) Survival Anglia/Rick Price,
(bottom) Ardea/François Gohier; p.158 B.&C. Alexander;
p.161 Bruce Coleman/Norbert Rosling; p.162–163 Survival
Anglia/Colin Willcock; p.163 Bruce Coleman/E.&P. Bauer; p.164
NHPA/Peter Johnson; p.165 B.&C. Alexander/Robert Estall.
Illustrations by Francis Mosley. Artworking by Claire Legemah.

Printed in Hong Kong

All words marked in **bold** can be found in the glossary.

CONTENTS

Mountains

LOOKING AT MOUNTAINS

High above the valleys and plains soar the mighty mountains of the world. Mountains come in many different shapes and sizes. They can be jagged, icy peaks; smoking **volcanoes**; or even green and fertile islands.

A wide and unique variety of animals, plants, and people has adapted to life on steep and rocky slopes. Some insects also live on mountain pastures. A few, like glacier fleas, can even live in ice and snow.

THE HEART OF THE EARTH

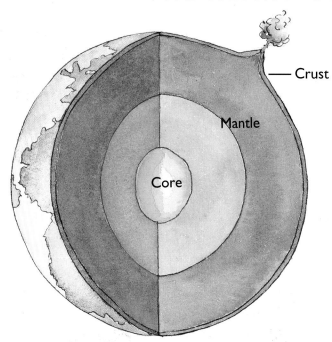

Crust

Mantle

Core

The earth is like an onion, made up of different layers of rock. The center, or **core**, is made up mostly of iron. The next layer is the **mantle**, a tightly packed band of rock about 1,800 miles (2,900 kilometers) thick. We live on the cool, outermost layer, or **crust**. This is up to 30 miles (50 kilometers) thick.

Near the earth's crust, the rocks of the mantle are hot and molten. This liquid rock, or lava, is squeezed from every side. Where the crust is weak, it spews out the lava and forms a type of mountain called a volcano.

Very few mountains rise alone from a plain. Usually they form part of a longer chain, or range, of mountains, such as the Andes, which run the length of the west coast of South America. As the earth's surface changes, new mountains form slowly over millions of years, and older ones gradually wear away.

This book mainly looks at the many different forms of life on the mighty mountains of the world.

▼ Mount Everest in the Himalaya is the highest peak on earth. It is 29,028 feet (8,848 meters) high. The Himalaya is the world's most recently formed mountain range. It is 1,500 miles (2,410 kilometers) long and 2,000 feet (6,000 meters) high, on average.

MAKING MOUNTAINS

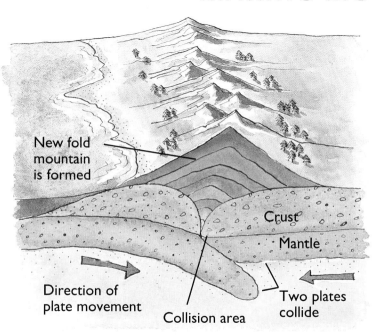

New fold mountain is formed

Crust

Mantle

Direction of plate movement

Two plates collide

Collision area

Large areas of the earth's crust, called **plates**, move slowly around on the earth's surface. The oceans and continents ride on the plates. Long ago, the plates were joined. Their edges could still fit together like pieces of a puzzle.

Sometimes the plates meet and grind together, causing earthquakes. At their edges, the rocks slowly fold upward to form **fold mountains** or drift apart to form valleys.

One plate may make the edge of another plate sink, while the rocks at its own edge rise very slowly to make a new range of mountains.

WHERE IN THE WORLD?

Any area of land that is higher than 1,000 feet (300 meters) above its surrounding flat land can be called mountainous. Mountains cover about one-fifth of the earth's surface. Australia and Africa have only a few mountains, while Asia has huge areas of mountainous land.

Vast mountains also form part of the ocean floor. Hawaii is the topmost part of an underwater volcano. Measured from the sea floor, it is higher than Mount Everest, at more than 29,500 feet (9,000 meters) tall.

Fault-block mountains have broad, flat tops, or **plateaus**. These mountains form when blocks of rock are forced up through cracks, or faults, in the crust by the liquid rock in the mantle. Rift valleys form when rock slides into a crack in the crust.

▼ This map shows the main mountain ranges. The younger ones, the Alps, the Rockies, the Andes, and the Himalaya, are fold mountains. The Scottish Highlands, the Atlas and Appalachian mountains, the Drakensberg, the Urals, and the Pyrenees are older and have been worn by the weather for millions of years.

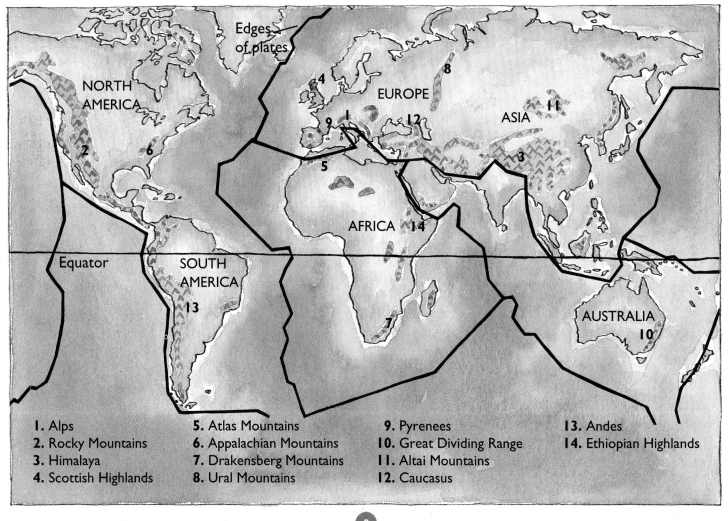

1. Alps
2. Rocky Mountains
3. Himalaya
4. Scottish Highlands
5. Atlas Mountains
6. Appalachian Mountains
7. Drakensberg Mountains
8. Ural Mountains
9. Pyrenees
10. Great Dividing Range
11. Altai Mountains
12. Caucasus
13. Andes
14. Ethiopian Highlands

◀ Mount Augustine is a live volcanic island off the coast of Alaska. In 1986, it erupted, and ash and gases spouted from its crater.

▼ Weird limestone mountains stand near the Guilin Li River in China. Limestone is soft and is worn away gradually by the wind or dissolved by rain. Over the years, these unusual mountains have been ground into strange shapes.

ICE, SNOW, AND RAIN

Mountains change all the time. Over the years, heavy rains soften their rocky outlines and gather to form rivers. These rivers eventually carve deep V-shaped channels or valleys into the side of the mountain.

Ice and snow also change the shape of mountains. There is less air high up a mountain to trap the warmth of the sun's rays, so it is very cold. Many of the world's peaks are covered with a deep blanket of snow and ice throughout the year.

▲ Sometimes snow gets too heavy and slips down the mountainside as an **avalanche**.

RAIN SHADOWS

Rain-filled clouds blow toward the land from the sea. They release their moisture when they reach cold mountain air. The landward side of a mountain receives little rain and is called the **rain shadow**.

▶ Ice may form slow-moving rivers called glaciers. Stones and rocks in the ice **erode**, or wear away, the mountains, leaving U-shaped channels, known as glaciated valleys. The glacier melts as it gets farther from the cold peak and into warmer areas. Shown here is the John Hopkins glacier in Alaska.

▼ Heavy rains often loosen the earth on a mountain and lead to a landslide. Strong winds also may blow away rocks and soil and change a mountain's shape. Sometimes heavy rocks and earth tumble down a mountainside, damaging buildings and injuring people.

TREES AND PLANTS

At high **altitudes**, it becomes harder for mountain plants to survive the cold and lack of water. Completely different plants grow on a protected sunny slope than on a slope exposed to icy winds.

In the Northern Hemisphere, both **deciduous** and **coniferous trees** grow on lower mountain slopes. Farther up, the deciduous trees thin out, and coniferous trees grow more thickly. Beyond, a few coniferous trees struggle to the **treeline**. Above this, conditions are too harsh for trees to grow. The height of the treeline varies with **latitude** and local weather patterns. Mountains away from the **equator** are colder and have lower treelines.

In tropical areas, dense rain forests grow lower down, while lush "cloud" forests of mossy **evergreen trees** grow farther up mountain slopes.

▲ A small ponderosa pine anchors itself in a boulder on a steep mountainside. The waxy needlelike leaves contain very little water to freeze and are shaped so that most snow will slide off the branches and not harm the tree.

◀ Cushions of grass, moss, and lichen grow on the thin soil and rock of upper slopes. At ground level, they are sheltered from the wind. All plant life stops at the **snowline**.

▶ In summer, the meadows high up in the European Alps are covered with a rich carpet of flowers. The plants must be sturdy to combat the cold and windy conditions. They are not very tall and their stems bend in the wind. Their roots hold them firmly in place. The petals are brightly colored to attract the few insects living there.

PLANT PANEL

In the Northern Hemisphere, deciduous and coniferous trees grow on lower slopes. Higher up, only coniferous trees survive. Once past the treeline, only shrubs, grasses, and flowers may grow on the thin mountain soil.

▼ The giant lobelia lives on Mount Kenya. It traps air in its hairs to keep warm. It grows up to 26 feet (8 meters) tall.

STAYING WARM

Mountain animals have long hair with a thick undercoat of fur to keep them warm. They are often larger than their relatives who live in valleys and plains. Some animals, like wild sheep and goats, feed on top pastures in summer and move downhill in winter. Smaller animals, like Alpine marmots and the mountain hares of Europe and Asia, feed mainly in top meadows. Marmots feed all summer and then **hibernate** for eight months and lose as much as one-quarter of their body fat.

Several **predators** stalk the mountains. In the Himalaya, rare snow leopards live near the snowline and prey on grazing animals. In Europe, hunters such as wolves and lynxes are seen occasionally.

▲ Mountain goats have hard, sharp hooves that grip the rock like pincers as they move about slippery top slopes to graze.

ANIMAL FACTS

● Pikas are found on European, Asian, and North American mountains. They feed on grasses and other plants. They spend the summer collecting stores of food to eat during the winter.

● The snow rabbit and the mountain hare both turn white in the winter so as to hide against the snow. This form of protection against predators is called **camouflage**.

▶ The cougar lives close to the snowline during the summer. Cougars, like brown bears and lynxes, prey on goats and other grazing animals.

▼ The Japanese macaque monkeys in the Shiga Highlands have learned to keep warm in the local hot springs. They cook their vegetables in the hot water before eating them. Here, one macaque checks another's fur for ticks and fleas.

FLYING AND HOPPING

The animals living on either side of a mountain range are often quite different from one another. Some birds and insects, however, manage to survive on either side. Birds must have thick feathers and strong lungs to be able to fly so high. Such specially equipped birds include the bar-headed goose, which migrates from Siberia to its distant wintering grounds in India.

The large birds of prey that live close to mountain peaks include the giant Andean condor, the lammergeier, and the golden eagle. There are also smaller birds that remain close to the ground, such as the chough in Europe and Asia, which feeds on insects, butterflies, and mountain plants.

FLYING HIGH

The Apollo butterfly lives on some of the highest mountains of Europe and Asia. It flies only when sunshine warms it. When the sun goes behind a cloud, the Apollo drops to the ground to save energy. The Apollo is now protected by law from butterfly collectors in most of its habitats in Europe.

◀ The mountain grasshopper has stiff flaps where its wings used to be. Those insects, like butterflies, that do still fly, stay near the ground so that they will not be blown away by the wind. Some insects even survive above the snowline.

▶ In the French Pyrenees, a male capercaillie struts about in the snow searching for a mate. Its call is a series of crackles and pops. The capercaillie mainly feeds on buds and cones.

▲ The lammergeier nests in mountain peaks. It is a large mountain vulture native to Europe, Asia, and Africa and mostly feeds on dead animals. Most other birds could not survive the cold.

▶ The hummingbirds of the high Andes become sluggish when it is cold at night. This is a red-tailed comet hummingbird.

MOUNTAIN DWELLERS

Lowland people get exhausted at high altitudes. There is little oxygen, and it is extremely cold. Mountain people have adapted to these harsh conditions. People such as the Bhotia of the Himalaya have enlarged hearts and lungs and wide nostrils so that their bodies may take in enough oxygen. They depend on sturdy yaks, members of the cattle family, to provide them with meat, wool, milk, transport, hides and butter.

In many areas, such as the Rocky Mountains, the European Alps, and Scandinavia, farmers rear dairy cattle and sheep in the mountains. The animals often are kept in barns on the valley floors to shelter them from the winter snows. In summer, they are herded to the higher pastures to be fattened on the rich grasses.

▲ An Afghan woman dressed in richly colored clothing milks her goat in the Hindu Kush.

▶ A lively market takes place in the Sherpa capital of Namche in Nepal. Sherpas farm, raised animals, and trade. They often act as guides and porters for mountaineering expeditions.

PEOPLE FACTS

● The Lapps are nomads who live in northern Sweden. Some Lapps keep reindeer to provide meat, milk, and skin for tents and clothes.

● The Andean Indians of South America keep llamas, vicunas, and alpacas. Some mine tin, copper, gold, and silver. Others grow barley and potatoes.

MOUNTAIN TREASURES

Valuable resources such as coal, metals such as copper, zinc, and iron ores, as well as semiprecious and precious minerals are mined from mountains. The bare rock itself is used by the building industry.

The banks of the Rocky Mountains in Canada are covered with useful softwoods, such as aspen, pine, and spruce. Hardwoods such as teak, ebony, mahogany, and rosewood grow on tropical mountains. Ships, furniture, and building materials are made from different types of wood.

Mountain rivers are often dammed to feed a reservoir of water. The rushing torrent turns huge turbines, which generate enough electricity to power whole cities or even nations, such as mountainous Switzerland.

▼ A dam is built on the Columbia River in Canada to store water for the use of city-dwellers.

▶ A loader piles logs onto the back of a trailer. When trees are felled on mountain slopes, the rain is no longer absorbed by the roots but runs freely, washing soil into the rivers. In the end, the slopes are left bare and eroded. With proper management, wood can be cut from special plantations.

◀ Emeralds are mined in the Andes in Colombia. The stones are cut and polished to make jewelry.

MOUNTAIN STOREHOUSE

Jewels, such as diamonds, rubies, emeralds, sapphires, quartz, gold, and platinum are taken from minerals and rocks found in mountains.

Granite and marble may be used in building banks, town halls, or palaces. Slate is used for making roofing tiles, and limestone is used to make cement.

Copper, zinc, and iron are extracted from mountain rocks. They are used in construction and sculpture and to make jewelry, tools, and utensils.

Softwoods are important for use in the construction of buildings, to make paper, and as fuel. Hardwoods are used to make long-lasting furniture.

MOUNTAINS IN DANGER

There are many threats to the mountains. Summer visitors can erode paths and crush rare plants. New ski resorts may scar whole mountainsides with cable cars and ski lifts.

Everywhere, mountain forests are being damaged. In many industrial nations, **acid rain** harms mountain forests. Cars and factories produce chemicals that pollute the rain. In Nepal, many trees are felled for fuel. Remaining tree roots cannot absorb enough rain water, so the fertile topsoil washes into the rivers, flooding them downstream. The mountain slopes are left bare, stripped down to their barren rock.

Mining can destroy a mountain, leaving only ugly waste. In Western Australia, entire mountains are dug away to remove their iron ore.

▲ In the Black Forest of southern Germany, mountain trees are poisoned by acid rain. The trees lose their leaves, wither, and die.

▶ This garbage was left by climbers on Mount Everest. Much of the garbage is plastic, which will never break down but will continue to blow around the mountainside for many years.

EROSION

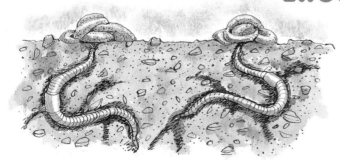

Earthworms help to wear down the mountains. Air and rain travel down the worms' tunnels and break down the rocks below. Fragments of rock come to the surface in the wormcasts and are washed away.

In 1900, forests covered 40 per cent of Ethiopia. Trees were felled, and crops and cattle eroded the bare earth. Today, trees cover only 4 per cent of mountainous Ethiopia, and there are often famines.

SAVING THE MOUNTAINS

In many countries, people have completely changed the nature of their local mountains. In Greece, for example, some forests have been cut down, and sheep and goats have eaten the remaining vegetation. The mountains are reduced to bare rock as the unprotected soil has been completely eroded by wind and rain.

Some countries have created national parks to protect their mountains. Forests are managed so that when one tree is cut down, another is planted. The habitats of wild animals, plants, and birds are protected from damage by people and industry. In this way, mountains can remain areas of great beauty.

All the world's mountains should be protected against long-lasting damage of mining, and logging and the erosion that follows. Mountains play an important role in the earth's weather patterns and support a unique variety of animals and plants.

▲ The yak, or grunting ox, lives on the slopes of the Himalaya in Nepal. These animals have long been used by local people for transport and as a supply of meat and milk. Local people must fight to preserve their traditional ways of life in the mountains.

◀ A volcano rises through the pearly dawn mist in East Java, Indonesia. New volcanoes are formed regularly along fault lines in the earth's crust, while old volcanoes cool and become extinct.

WHAT YOU CAN DO

Support ecology campaigns in these ways:

● There are many groups that campaign to protect mountains and other endangered areas. Find out about their work from magazines and newspapers, on the radio, or on television.

● Tell your friends and relatives about acid rain and mountains in danger.

● Write to your legislators and ask them to fight to protect mountains and help prevent acid rain.

When you go walking or climbing in the mountains, follow these essential rules:

● Use only the marked paths.

● Never pick wild flowers.

● Try not to tread on any plants growing on the mountainside.

HOW COYOTE STOLE FIRE

For thousands of years people have told stories about the world around them. Often these stories try to explain something that people do not understand, like how the world began. This story, told by Native Americans, tries to explain how fire was discovered at the top of a volcanic mountain.

Long ago, when the world was young, Coyote passed by the camp where the People lived. The midday sun was shining on the first snow of winter, and all the People were huddled together in their chilly teepees. It was far too cold to venture out into the world.

"If only we could keep just a little piece of the warm summer sun in our teepees in the winter," said one, wrapping his thick blanket around him more tightly against the draught. He sneezed and looked miserable.

Coyote pitied the People. His own fur grew thick and warm during the winter. Then Coyote had an idea. Perhaps he could help them!

Coyote traveled all the next day to the very top of a nearby mountain. There, in a huddle, sat three fiery creatures, guarding a tiny fire.

As Coyote approached, the three fiery creatures began to sniff the mountain air and look around them suspiciously. They chattered,

"Who's that? Who's trying to steal our fire? Go away!"

When they saw Coyote, the three fiery creatures began to hiss loudly. They stretched out their fiery fingers toward him until he was forced to back off. Then they settled down around the fire again.

But Coyote had not gone very far. He ran off a little way and then crept back and hid behind some bushes to keep watch.

The three fiery creatures spent the whole day guarding the fire but, as night began to fall, two of them disappeared into a nearby cave. A few hours later, the creature left by the fire went to the mouth of the cave and called out to the others.

The second creature soon came out to take his place. Later, the second creature went to the mouth of the cave and called out. This time there was no reply. He called again but still got no answer. Finally, he went right inside the cave, and the fire was left unguarded for a few minutes before the third creature came out.

Coyote watched all this with interest. In fact, he sat watching the fiery creatures for three whole days and nights. Every day, the fire was guarded all the time, except for a few minutes of the night when all three fiery creatures went inside the cave. This was his one chance.

On the fourth night Coyote was ready. When the second fiery creature went into the cave to wake up the third, he ran toward the fire, picked up a flaming branch in his jaws, and dashed off down the steep side of the mountain.

As he ran, he heard the sounds of screaming behind him. The fiery creatures had discovered their loss and were now chasing after him.

Coyote ran and ran, but the fiery creatures were much faster than him. At last one of them came near enough to grab at Coyote's tail. He snatched at it with his fiery hand and scorched the tip of Coyote's tail white. To this day, all coyotes have a white tip to their tails.

When Coyote felt the fiery fingers on his tail, he tossed the flaming branch high into the air. Squirrel leapt down from a tree, grabbed the branch, and ran off down the mountain with it. The fiery creatures followed.

Still they ran too fast. Squirrel felt their burning breath on her back, singeing her fur. To this day, her tail curls up from the scorching heat.

Squirrel threw the branch to Chipmunk, who ran on down the mountain with the fiery creatures close behind.

It took only a few minutes before the fiery creatures began to gain on Chipmunk. He felt the fiery claw of one of them grab at his back, but he wriggled away. And to this day, chipmunks have stripes down their backs from the fiery claw-marks.

Reaching the bottom of the mountain, Chipmunk threw the burning branch to Frog. Poor Frog could not run very fast at all. The fiery beings swept down on him, and one of them grabbed him by the tail. But with one enormous leap, Frog jumped out of the creature's hand, leaving his tail behind. To this day, frogs have no tails.

As soon as he had put some distance between himself and the fiery creatures, Frog threw the flaming branch across to Wood, who swallowed it whole.

The fiery creatures did not know what to do. They were desperate and kicked and scratched and bit at Wood, but he refused to give back their fire. They sat near Wood for four whole days before giving up.

But Coyote knew how to get the fire out of Wood. He taught the People how to twist a stick between their hands with the pointed end rubbing a hole in a piece of wood until a spark appeared. Then the People learned to feed the spark with dry grass until they had a flame. The People could now warm themselves and would never need to be cold again.

TRUE OR FALSE?

Which of these facts are true and which ones are false?
If you have read this book carefully, you will know the answers.

1. The outer layer of the earth is called the mantle.

2. The earth's plates once fitted together like a giant jigsaw puzzle.

3. Mountains cover about half of the earth's surface.

4. Land on a mountainside facing away from the sea often receives very little rain.

5. Alpine flowers are often dull in color to attract local insects.

6. Trees can only survive up to the treeline on the slopes of a mountain.

7. Marmots hibernate all year around and lose most of their body weight.

8. The macaque monkeys of Japan have learned how to cook their food in hot water springs.

9. The Lapps of northern Sweden keep yaks to provide transport, food, and skins.

10. Emeralds are used to make jewelry because of their rich red color.

11. Another name for the grunting ox is the yak.

Deserts

LOOKING AT THE DESERTS

There are places where rain hardly ever falls and few plants can survive, where the sun scorches the earth and strong winds whip sand and dust from the ground. These places are called **deserts**. But not all deserts are areas of shifting sands and intense heat. In fact, rock and gravel cover the greater part of most deserts. Some deserts, such as the Gobi Desert in Asia, are actually cold for most of the year. Other deserts are blisteringly hot during the day, but temperatures drop dramatically during the night.

A surprising variety of plant and animal life struggles to survive the harsh conditions of the desert, and many people call it their home.

DID YOU KNOW?

The scientific definition of a desert is "a place that has very little vegetation and receives less than 10 inches (25 centimeters) of rain each year." This means that the land mass at the South Pole could be called a desert, because it receives only a few inches (centimeters) of rain each year. The water does not fall as rain, however, but snow!

▶ Some of the highest sand dunes in the world can be found in the Namib Desert in southern Africa. Sand dunes are not fixed features of the desert. They are mobile mounds of sand that are shaped by the wind.

▼ Death Valley, California, is the hottest, driest area of the United States.

▼ A boulder-strewn part of the Namib Desert shows signs of life after a good year's rainfall.

WHERE IN THE WORLD?

Deserts cover about one-fifth of all the land in the world. There are deserts in parts of Africa, Asia, Australia, and North and South America.

Most deserts lie along two imaginary lines north and south of the equator, called the **Tropic of Cancer** and the **Tropic of Capricorn**. Here, and in other desert regions, dry air currents blow across the land. These dry air currents can blow hot or cold, but they rarely carry rain clouds. Consequently the lands they cross are starved of rain and given no protection from the sun.

This map shows the main desert areas of the world. Do you live near desert lands?

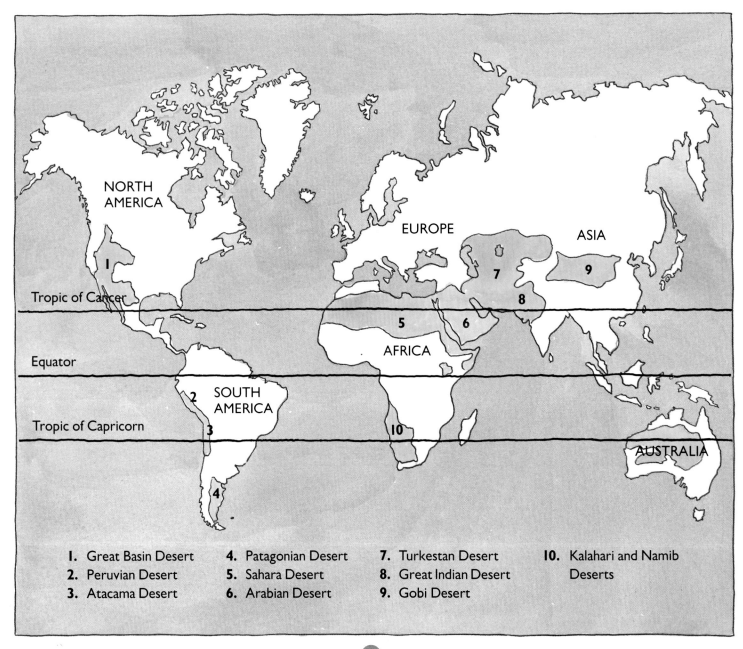

1. Great Basin Desert	4. Patagonian Desert	7. Turkestan Desert	10. Kalahari and Namib Deserts
2. Peruvian Desert	5. Sahara Desert	8. Great Indian Desert	
3. Atacama Desert	6. Arabian Desert	9. Gobi Desert	

RAIN SHADOWS

Some deserts are called rain shadow deserts. These occur where large mountains block the path of rain-bearing wind. The raised mountain ground pushes the wind upward and as it rises, it cools. The drop in temperature causes clouds carried by the wind to burst and release their rain. The wind continues over the mountains, but by the time it reaches the other side it carries no rain clouds. This natural process creates some of the world's wettest environments—rain forests—alongside the world's driest.

● The Sahara in northern Africa is the largest desert in the world. It covers an area roughly the size of the United States.

● The Gobi Desert in eastern Asia is situated on high, windy plains. It is the coldest desert in the world.

● Nearly half of Australia is covered by desert.

● The Arabian Desert is the sandiest desert in the world.

● The smallest desert regions of the world are the Peruvian and Atacama deserts on the western coast of South America.

● Many of the world's deserts are bordered by areas of scant vegetation. These **scrublands** would become true deserts if they were to lose their native trees and plants.

▲ Ancient rock paintings in African and Asian deserts show giraffes, antelope, and other grazing animals that could not survive in today's desert conditions. This suggests that the lands were once more **fertile**. Evidence of ancient lakes and forests can also be found in the world's deserts.

DESERT PLANTS

It is astonishing that any plants have learned to survive in desert conditions. Most plants rely on regular rainfall, but desert plants may have to go without fresh water for more than a year. In addition, many desert plants have to cope with both hot and cold temperatures, as each boiling day turns into another freezing night.

Some desert plants remain hidden in the ground as seeds until rain falls. By waiting until conditions are good, they do not have to cope with the rigors of desert life.

▼ The gigantic welwitschia plant is unique to the Namib Desert. This desert has a rare water source—fogs that drift across it from the coast. The welwitschia's leaves absorb tiny particles of water from the foggy air.

▲ Cacti are the most famous desert plants. They are native to North and South American deserts, but they have been introduced to other parts of the world.

Prickly pear cacti were taken to Australia and planted as hedges around homes in the outback. They grew so quickly that large areas were overrun by the spiky plants. Small creatures that eat the prickly pear's soft insides had to be introduced to Australia to help reclaim the land.

▶ Cacti are flowering plants. Some cacti produce flowers every year, while others rarely come into blossom. Birds visit cacti to extract sugary nectar from their flowers or search their stems for insects.

The cactus in this picture is a giant saguaro. Saguaro cacti can grow to nearly 50 feet (15 meters) in height and may hold several tons (kilograms) of water in their swollen stems. Like other cacti, the saguaro has no leaves. Instead, prickly spines grow around its stem. These spines create a layer of still air around the surface of the plant and so protect it from drying winds.

SURVIVAL TRICKS

Desert plants have special ways of surviving without regular rainfall. Some suck up as much water as they can during occasional rains and then store it in their stems or leaves. Here are some other ways desert plants collect and conserve water.

Some desert trees have long **taproots**, which grow deep into the ground to reach underground water sources.

Many plants, like the creosote bush, have a vast network of shallow roots to extract every available drop of moisture from their patch of the desert.

Some desert plants store food and water underground in thickened roots, bulbs, or **tubers**. The stems of such plants, exposed to sun and wind, may look dead, but as soon as it rains they spring into life, producing leaves, fruits, and flowers.

HIDDEN LIFE

It is difficult to believe that hundreds of different animals live in deserts. Most of the time, these are quiet, still places. This is because many desert creatures move around only at dawn or dusk. At other times of the day, they burrow underground or hide beneath rocks or plants to avoid very hot or cold conditions.

The animals living in the desert rely on plant life and on each other for their survival. Roots, stems, leaves, and seeds form the basic diet of many desert creatures, and they, in turn, are hunted by other animals. The largest hunters in the desert include wild cats, foxes, and wolves.

Some desert creatures get all the water they need from the food they eat. Others have to travel long distances to visit rare water holes.

▲ Scorpions hunt spiders, insects, and other small animals on the desert floor. Once they have caught their meal, they use the poisonous stings at the end of their tails to kill their prey. People stung by a scorpion usually suffer just a sharp pain, but the most powerful scorpion stings can be deadly.

▼ Many reptiles are successful desert dwellers, especially snakes and lizards. Some snakes have a special way of moving across shifting sands. They throw their heads to one side and their bodies follow in a loop. This is called sidewinding. Snakes can also burrow into the sand to cool down or escape from predators.

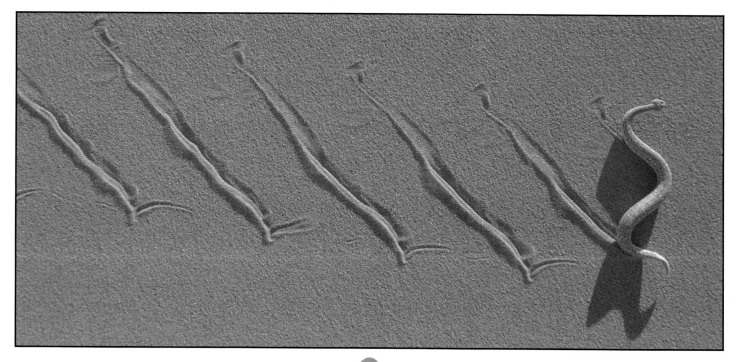

▶ Rabbits, gerbils, and many other small mammals live in desert lands. The cottontail rabbit, right, can be found in some American deserts. It has large ears that act as radiators, giving off heat and so helping the rabbit to cool down.

▼ Many lizards live in the world's deserts. Like other reptiles, they have a scaly skin that stops them from drying up in the baking sunshine. Most lizards are insect-eaters. They chase flies or sit patiently waiting for a beetle or a line of ants to pass them by. Lizards have many enemies, so they must stay on their guard. The horned lizard, below, has excellent camouflage that makes it hard to find on the desert floor.

CROSSING THE DESERT

The largest desert animals do not remain in one area of the desert. They travel long distances in search of food and water. Small numbers of antelope, goats, and sheep are found in most deserts of the world. A rare horse, called Przewalski's horse, once roamed the cold Gobi Desert but is now thought to be **extinct** in the wild.

The most famous animal to cross the desert is the camel. The camel is sometimes called the ship of the desert, because it can travel over vast seas of inhospitable rock and sand better than any other animal.

There are two kinds of camels. The dromedary has one hump on its back and a thin coat. It is native to the hot deserts of Arabia and North Africa, but it also has been introduced to parts of America and Australia. The Bactrian camel has two humps and a darker, thicker coat than its cousin. It comes from the cooler central Asian deserts.

Camels are well built for desert life. They have bushy eyebrows and two rows of eyelashes to help keep the sand out of their eyes. Their slit nostrils can be closed for the same reason. Their two-toed feet spread out as they walk and stop them from sinking into the sand.

The humps on camels' backs do not contain water as was once believed. They hold fat reserves that can be broken down into food when camels are crossing the desert. If a camel is starving, its hump will shrink.

DID YOU KNOW?

● Less than 100 years ago, it was impossible to cross the vast Sahara and Arabian deserts without the help of a camel. Today cars and trucks are used for many desert journeys, and camels are becoming less important to the lives of desert people.

● Thirsty camels can drink up to 30 gallons (140 liters) of water in one sitting and then go for more than a week without water.

● Camels are the domestic animals of the desert. They are used as transportation. They provide meat and milk for food. Their hairy coats are woven into cloth. Even the camel's dry droppings are used as fuel for cooking fires.

WHEN WATER FALLS

Some deserts have regular rainy seasons, but others may not see rain for many years. In the desert there are only torrential downpours. Violent desert rainstorms cause flash floods and destruction. Plants are washed away, and some animals drown.

Rain brings life as well as death to desert lands. Days after a heavy storm, billions of tiny seeds spring to life on the desert floor. These small flowering plants, called **ephemerals**, have been hiding in the sand since the last rainfall. Millions of insect eggs are also brought to life by the drumming rain, and so an army of flies, bees, and wasps appears. These insects feed on the ephemerals and help them to reproduce by spreading pollen from flower to flower.

Eight weeks after the rain, the desert is empty again. The colorful flowers and buzzing insects have gone. But millions and billions of new seeds and eggs now lie hidden in the desert sands. Many of them will be eaten by permanent desert dwellers, but some are bound to survive until the next rain comes and the life cycle can be repeated.

▶ Lightning strikes as a storm passes over the Sonoran Desert in North America. A whole year's rainfall can come in one single cloudburst.

▲ Colorful, flowering plants brighten the sandy Arabian Desert after a recent rainfall.

DID YOU KNOW?

● Sometimes rainstorms fail to wet the desert floor. If it is very hot when a storm occurs, the rain may turn into vapor before it reaches the ground. More than 12 inches (30 centimeters) of rain may fall during one heavy storm in the desert.

● The Atacama Desert is the driest in the world. Some parts of it experienced a 400-year drought until 1971.

DESERT PEOPLE

The desert is a dangerous place for people not used to its hostile conditions. Even so, a few people call the open desert home.

The **Bushmen** of the Kalahari Desert in southern Africa are **nomads**, which means that they travel from place to place. Bushmen survive by hunting wild game and gathering edible plants and insects. Some Aborigines once lived this way in the heart of Australia's desert lands, but most are now settled in goverment-funded camps.

The world's most barren deserts such as the Sahara, Arabian, and Gobi deserts do not have enough native plants and animals to support **hunter-gatherers**. Instead, the nomadic people take from the desert what they can but also kill or trade animals such as goats, sheep, or camels for food.

PEOPLE FACTS

Bushmen rarely drink. They get most of the water they need from plant roots and desert melons found on or under the desert floor.

The turban worn by many desert people is not a hat. It is a very long piece of cloth that is wrapped around and around the head. It helps to keep desert sand out of the eyes, nose, and mouth.

People in the cold Gobi Desert live in sturdy, round huts called yurts. These simple homes can withstand winds up to 90 miles (145 kilometers) an hour.

► These men belong to a group of people called the Tuareg. The Tuareg were once known as the pirates of the desert. For many years they controlled trade across the Sahara by patrolling the desert on racing camels.

◄ A Bushman of the Kalahari makes a fire by rubbing two sticks together. Bushmen have their own special language that includes clicking sounds. Bushmen live in huts built from local materials. The frame is made of branches, and the roof is thatched with long grass.

▼ Many desert nomads live in tents, like the one in this picture. When it is time to move on, the nomads pack up the tent. It is then carried by a camel or donkey.

DESERT OASES

In parts of the desert, plants grow in abundance and water is available throughout the year. These places are called oases.

Most oases are fed by underground pools of water that formed over thousands of years. The water is trapped between layers of rock below the desert floor. Rivers also create oases. The largest oasis in the world lies along the banks of the great River Nile, which flows through the Sahara.

Oases are the most densely populated areas of the desert. The regular water supply makes it possible for people to settle permanently and build villages, towns, or cities. The land is **irrigated**, and date palms, olives, wheat, millet, and other food crops are grown.

▲ If seasonal rains fail, water must be carried to the fields to keep desert crops alive.

▶ Many desert towns are built from materials of the desert itself. Mud is mixed with straw and water to make bricks, which are then baked in the sun. This village is the home of the Dogon. Dogon people get their water from nearby mountain pools. The Dogons live in Mali, which is in northern Africa.

▼ Oases are like green islands surrounded by a sea of sand and rock. Animals and people alike depend on oases for their drinking water.

Oases do not last forever. The world's deserts are littered with ghost towns, where the water has run dry or the oasis has been swamped by shifting sand dunes. In such places the people have moved on.

CREEPING DESERTS

The world's deserts are growing. Through a process known as **desertification**, scrub and grasslands become as dry and barren as the deserts they border. At the present rate of desertification, more than 77,220 square miles (200,000 square kilometers) of new desert land throughout the world are created every year.

Deserts naturally shrink and grow depending on the amount of rain they receive. In recent years, however, widespread droughts have caused deserts to grow at an alarming rate.

Scientists believe the droughts are part of a worldwide change in weather patterns caused by pollution in the atmosphere.

Desert nomads speed up the process of desertification by cutting down trees and grazing their animals on threatened grasslands. This leaves the land exposed to sun, wind, and occasional violent rains. The delicate **topsoil** dries out then is blown and washed away.

Intensive farming can also cause desertification. The pressure to grow

more and more food on the same amount of land encourages farmers to overwork the soil, and this can have disastrous consequences. In the 1930's, intensive farming and grazing in America's southern states created a huge area of bare and desertlike land called the Dust Bowl. Droughts had dried up the soil, and winds then carried it away. Cities hundreds of miles away were plunged into darkness as huge clouds of dust blew across the sky.

▼ If the ground cover is removed from dry scrublands, the hot sun bakes the earth. Rains run straight off the hard ground, and any remaining trees weaken and die.

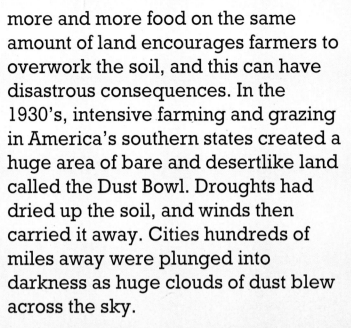

DID YOU KNOW?

More than 400 million short tons (363 million metric tons) of African soil is blown west over the Atlantic Ocean every year. In 1988 hundreds of tiny, pink Saharan frogs rained down on a British village during a bad storm.

DESERTS TODAY

For centuries the world's deserts were regarded as terrifying wastelands. They remained the exclusive property of small desert tribes who managed to survive in hostile conditions. Only recently has the arrival of cars, trucks, and airplanes expanded the possibilities for desert exploration.

Today industries are active in the desert. Mining companies use massive machinery to extract rich mineral reserves such as copper, iron, salt, and uranium. Oil is also found in some deserts and has brought great wealth to certain areas. Saudi Arabia holds some of the world's largest oil fields.

Elsewhere, modern technology has been used to turn the desert green. By finding new underground water sources or by tapping nearby rivers, people can grow crops on desert lands.

Desertification is a problem in many areas of the world, but Africa is the most obvious victim. In some African countries, crops have failed for several years running, which has caused widespread **famine**. Many nomads have cast off their ancient ways of life, as lengthy droughts have left the desert bare.

◀ As rich countries transform their deserts into farmland, poorer African countries try to hold back the creeping edge of the Sahara. This man is building simple rock walls to prevent the seasonal rains from running straight off the hard ground.

DID YOU KNOW?

● Today **arid** lands produce one-fifth of the world's food supply. By 2000, one-third of all farmland may be desert if the soil is overworked.

● Satellite pictures can locate hidden water pools under the desert floor. Modern drilling equipment can then reach the water to create new oases.

▲ Oil flares send smoke plumes into the desert air.

▶ Plastic tunnels cover healthy desert crops. The tunnels prevent precious water from **evaporating** into the dry desert air. Continual evaporation may encourage salts to rise to the surface of the desert. These salts kill most plant life and poison the soil.

JEALOUS GOOMBLE-GUBBON

For thousands of years people have told stories about the world around them. Often these stories try to explain something that people do not really understand, like how the world began or where light comes from. This tale is told by the Aboriginal people of Australia.

Long ago in Australia was the Dream Time when everything was made. The land was made, with mountains, plains, and valleys full of all sorts of animals, birds, and plants. And the sea was made, full of whales, dolphins, and plants. But there were not yet any fish.

All the birds had been given wonderful and extraordinary voices: Crow croaked his rasping caw, Kookaburra laughed her hilarious chuckle, and the other birds sang in all their different voices. They sat singing in the trees and bushes all day long, because they were so happy.

When I say they all had wonderful and extraordinary voices, I am forgetting Goomble-Gubbon, the turkey. Goomble-Gubbon could only make a low bubbling noise in his throat, which sounded like this: "goomble gubbon, goomble gubbon." All the other birds thought Goomble-Gubbon's voice was a great joke, and they sang even more beautifully when he was around just to tease him.

Of course, they didn't really mean to be cruel. They were all so happy themselves that they did not realize how much they were hurting poor Goomble-Gubbon's feelings. They were very fond of him in spite of his bad-tempered ways.

Goomble-Gubbon did not find his voice funny. He thought it was terrible, and he was very jealous of all the other birds' voices. He tried everything he could to improve his voice, but nothing was any use. If only the other birds' voices were not so wonderful and extraordinary, his voice would not seem so terrible, he thought.

One day was worse than ever before. The other birds had been laughing at Goomble-Gubbon all morning, and he was tired of it. So he went off to visit his friend Lizard. Lizard never laughed at his voice. The two of them sat talking and telling stories until the sun began to set. Just then, Kookaburra flew into the branches of a nearby tree and began to laugh.

Now, Kookaburra could not help laughing. She laughed at everything, even at things that were not at all funny, and Goomble-Gubbon should have known this really. But he was fed up with being teased by all the other birds, and so he thought that Kookaburra had flown over and perched on that very branch just to laugh at him.

"What do you think you're laughing at?" he snapped angrily.

Kookaburra looked most surprised and flew off to tell the other birds about Goomble-Gubbon's strange behavior.

Meanwhile Goomble-Gubbon made up his mind to put a stop to the other birds' teasing once and for all. He waited until it was dark and all the birds were asleep in the trees. Then, very quietly, he went to the magic burning tree. This was a tree where men took their firesticks to fetch fire for food, warmth, and light for their camps. Goomble-Gubbon picked up a stick from the ground and lit it from the tree. Then he crept around to all the trees and bushes where the birds were sleeping and set the bottom branches alight.

"That should get rid of those nasty laughing birds," he thought to himself gleefully. "Now I'll have the most beautiful voice of all."

However, Kookaburra was not asleep. She heard Goomble-Gubbon creeping around beneath the trees and woke the other birds to warn them.

A great swarm of birds rose up from the trees, screeching and crying. The birds who could fly fast flew away as quickly as they could to far-off places where there was no fire. Those who could not fly fast enough to get away from the flames flew into the sea to cool off. As they entered the water, their wings turned into fins and their feathers became scales. At last there were fish in the sea!

Goomble-Gubbon was furious that his plan had not worked. He waved the firestick wildly, but he managed only to singe his own feathers a nasty smoky color and burn his head bright red too. He threw the firestick far out into the bush.

The fire in the trees went on burning until the land in the center of Australia was quite barren and dry. And that is how the desert came to be in the center of Australia. All because of jealous Goomble-Gubbon.

TRUE OR FALSE?

Which of these facts are true and which ones are false? If you have
read this book carefully, you will know the answers.

1. All deserts are very hot.

2. Deserts receive no rain at all during the year.

3. The Gobi Desert is the largest desert in the world.

4. Nights in the desert are extremely cold.

5. Lush rain forests can lie alongside rain shadow deserts.

6. Saguaro cacti can grow close to 50 feet (15 meters) high.

7. The ears of the American cottontail rabbit act as radiators.

8. A camel's humps are used to store water.

9. The dromedary has two humps and a thick coat.

10. The Tuareg were once known as the pirates of the desert.

11. Many desert towns are built from mud bricks.

12. In 1988 thousands of large blue fish rained down on a British village during a bad storm.

Oceans

LOOKING AT THE OCEANS

More than two-thirds of the world's surface is covered by vast oceans. The oceans are the oldest and largest living **environments**. Life began here more than 3,500 million years ago. Without the fertile oceans, the earth would be dry, barren, and devoid of life.

Beneath the oceans lie rugged mountains, active volcanoes, vast plateaus, and almost bottomless **trenches**. The deepest ocean trenches could easily swallow up the tallest mountains found on land.

Seen from above, the oceans appear empty and unchanging, but beneath the surface hides a unique world where water takes the place of air. A fantastic and rich assortment of plants and animals lives in these waters, from microscopic **plankton** to the giant blue whale.

DID YOU KNOW?

● Salt is not the only substance found in seawater. There are also tiny traces of gold, silver, uranium, and other valuable **minerals**.

● Sound travels through water five times faster than through air. Some sea animals such as dolphins navigate through the oceans by bouncing sounds off their surroundings and listening to their **echoes**.

● Although oceans dominate the world map, we have only just begun to explore its hidden depths. The deepest part of the ocean was first visited in 1960.

▶ There are no boundaries in the ocean. Animals can travel freely through the water. Most sea animals breathe underwater, but some, like the dolphin and whale, need to come up for air every few minutes.

◀ In the tropics the ocean is warm and clear, but around the North and South poles it is very cold; here, parts of the ocean are frozen all year long. Huge chunks of ice called icebergs float in these seas.

DIVIDING THE SEAS

In truth there is only one ocean. It stretches from the North Pole to the South Pole and encircles the globe. However, because the **continents** loosely divide the water, four separate oceans are recognized—the Pacific, the Atlantic, the Indian, and the Arctic. Within these oceans are smaller bodies of water called seas, **bays**, and **gulfs** that are cut off from the open ocean by land formations.
The Pacific is the largest and deepest of the four great oceans. It covers more of the world's surface than all of the continents put together. The word *pacific* means peaceful, but the water can be very rough. Waves higher than 112 feet (35 meters) tall have been recorded in the Pacific Ocean.

The Atlantic is the second biggest ocean and the busiest. Boats regularly cross the Atlantic waters carrying cargo between the Americas, Africa, and countries in Europe.

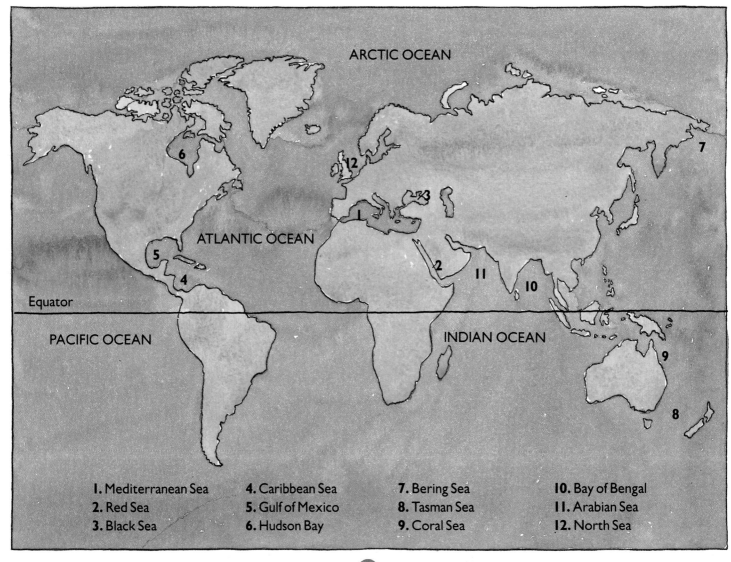

1. Mediterranean Sea	4. Caribbean Sea	7. Bering Sea	10. Bay of Bengal
2. Red Sea	5. Gulf of Mexico	8. Tasman Sea	11. Arabian Sea
3. Black Sea	6. Hudson Bay	9. Coral Sea	12. North Sea

DID YOU KNOW?

● One drop of seawater may travel through all the world's oceans in 5,000 years.

● The Atlantic Ocean is growing and the Pacific Ocean is shrinking. The world's continents move a few inches (centimeters) each year. So, the relative sizes of the oceans are always changing.

● Greek divers are known to have reached depths of 75 to 100 feet (22 to 30.5 meters) in search of sponges, coral, and other treasures. When a diver ran short of breath, he would poke his head into a special weighted diving bell filled with air from the surface.

● In several countries around the world the legend is told of a lost continent called Atlantis. This land is supposed to have lain in the Atlantic Ocean and was allegedly swallowed up by the sea after earthquakes and floods.

▲ In warm, tropical seas where the water is shallow and clear, there are vast, rocky structures known as coral reefs. These are the handiwork of small sea animals called polyps. Coral reefs are the marine equivalent of rain forests. They hold a greater variety of life than any other part of the oceans.

MOVING WAVES

The world's oceans are always on the move. They travel in well-defined circular patterns called ocean **currents**. The currents flow like rivers, carrying warm water from the tropics and cold water from the Poles. Where two currents meet, the colder water sinks, pushing warmer water up to the surface.

Besides the ocean currents, there is also the regular movement of the **tides**. Twice a day, all around the world, the oceans rise and fall along the coastlines. Scientists do not fully understand how the tides work, but they know they are linked to the pull on the earth by the moon and the sun. The continual movement of the oceans is important to marine life. The tides and currents carry food from one part of the ocean to another. They stir up the water and produce small bubbles of oxygen, which the ocean animals need to breathe.

In the northern hemisphere the ocean currents travel in a clockwise direction. In the southern hemisphere they travel counterclockwise. The wind is the driving force behind the ocean's currents.

OCEAN POWER

Giant whirlpools or maelstroms can occur where two rushing currents are forced through narrow channels. These turbulent waters can destroy small sailing vessels.

Earthquakes and volcanic eruptions under the surface of the ocean can cause huge waves to speed through the water and explode on the shore. These giant waves are often called tidal waves, but their proper name is tsunamis.

FOOD FOR LIFE

Plants provide the basic food for life in the ocean, just as they do on land. Plants that grow underwater are called algae, and there are two main groups found in the oceans.

The most familiar ocean algae are the seaweeds found around our coastlines. Limpets, periwinkles, and other shoreline creatures graze on seaweeds, but these are not available to the animals of the open ocean.

The most important marine plants are called phytoplankton. These tiny, floating plants grow wherever sunlight goes through the water. Huge clouds of phytoplankton drift in the upper layers of the ocean, but they are too small to be seen without a microscope.

Floating alongside and feeding upon the phytoplankton are tiny animals called zooplankton. This rich mix of plant and animal life, called plankton, is the foundation of all marine life.

PLANKTON FACTS

● Sailors crossing the ocean at night often see a soft glow on the water's surface. This is because some plankton produce flashes of blue-green light when they are disturbed.

● The very first lifeforms probably looked similar to today's phytoplankton.

● The largest animals in the world feed on plankton. Blue whales can weigh more than 81.7 short tons (90 metric tons) and measure more than 100 feet (30.48 meters) long. They sieve krill, tiny plankton animals, from the ocean waters through a curtain of whalebone inside their mouths.

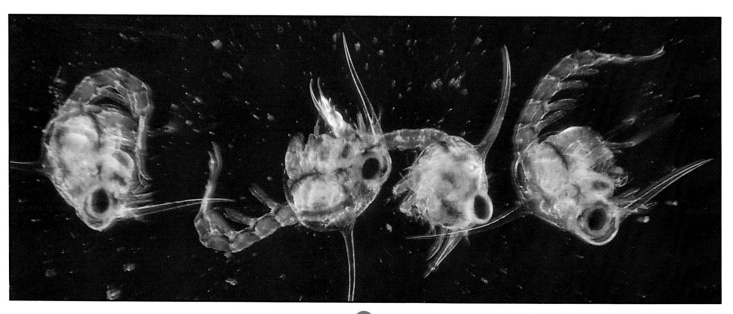

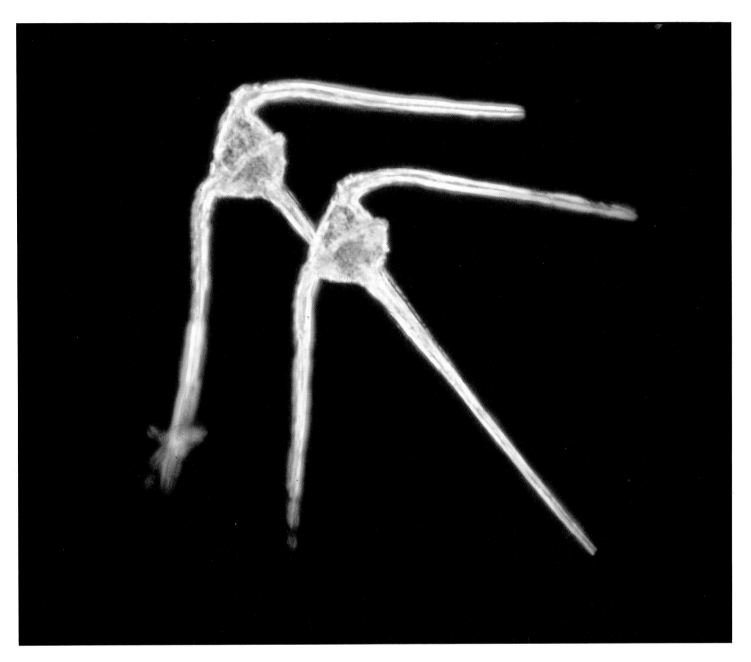

▲ ▶ Many of the tiny floating plants that make up phytoplankton join together to make chains and bracelets. Others float alone and look like small pill boxes, sea shells, pencils, ice picks, or ribbons.

◀ Some members of zooplankton are simple, single-celled lifeforms, but many are the tiny offspring of fish, crabs, starfish, and other sea animals.

ALL SHAPES AND SIZES

There is a staggering variety of animals living in the oceans. The size, shape, and color of these animals change enormously. To some extent, each marine animal's appearance depends on its lifestyle and where in the ocean it lives. Sea anemones and sponges, for instance, stay rooted to the ocean floor for their entire lives and look more like plants than animals.

Fish are the most familiar marine creatures, but even their looks can be deceptive. Some species, like eels and pipefish, look more like worms or snakes than fish. Others, like the delicate sea horse, seem like a different sort of animal altogether.

▲ Many sea animals are transparent or a silver-blue color, but some have bright, bold markings. The most colorful animals live in clear tropical waters. Their striking appearance helps them to establish territory and frighten off would-be attackers.

◀ The octopus is one of many curious sea animals. It has eight arms and a short, rounded body. Many octopuses live on the ocean floor, where they hide among rocks and grab passing animals with their long suckered arms. To swim, octopuses squirt water from a special siphon in their bodies.

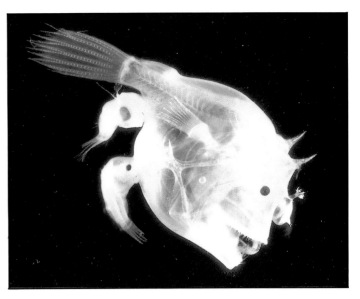

▲ It is cold, black, and very still in the deepest parts of the ocean. Many animals living there have a light on their bodies that they use to attract prey. The deep-sea angler fish, above, is very strange. If the male of the species meets his mate, he attaches himself to her body. After. a time, his body breaks down and he is used to fertilize the female's eggs.

▲ Sponges encrust rocks, corals, and vegetation on the sea floor, from the shallowest coastlines to the deepest trenches. There are more than 3,500 marine sponges. Some form fleshy sheets; others form upright chimney stacks. Sponges sieve dead and decaying matter from the water around them.

▶ The blue-spotted stingray is a close relative of the shark. It floats over the surface of the seabed feeding on slugs, worms, and other sea animals.

THE HUNTER AND THE HUNTED

Many marine animals spend their entire lives sifting the water for plankton; but they, in turn, are hunted by other animals. It is estimated that for every 10 plankton-feeders at least one hunter lurks nearby.

One of the most notorious marine hunters is the shark. Sharks have a reputation as man-eaters, but of the 200 varieties only 25 are in fact dangerous to people. Sharks are perfect killing machines. Their bodies are streamlined for a fast-moving, hunting life, and their mouths are lined with razor-sharp teeth.

Not all marine hunters are as fearsome as the sharks. The pretty sea anemones look harmless, but they trap animals in their feathery tentacles and inject poison into their victims' bodies.

DEFENSE FACTS

Octopuses and cuttlefish squirt ink into the face of their attacker. This gives them time to get away.

Flying fish leap out of the water to escape their enemies.

Many sea animals, like clams and oysters, live in shells. The shells provide a home and act as armor, protecting the animals' soft bodies.

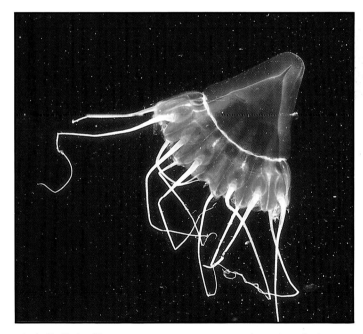

▲ Jellyfish, like sea anemones, catch animals in their trailing tentacles and then poison them. Some of the most powerful poisons in the natural world are produced by jellyfish.

◄ Sharks race through the water, chasing their prey of fish, seals, turtles, small whales, other sharks, and even sea birds. Even when they are not chasing their next meal, sharks must keep moving at all times or they begin to sink.

TAKING TO THE WATER

During the long passage of time, a small procession of land animals have returned to the oceans for their livelihoods. Reptiles, mammals, and even birds have braved the deep, salty waters to take advantage of the rich bounty of sea life.

Whales, seals, turtles, and penguins are some of the animals that have left dry land to colonize the oceans. These creatures cannot breathe underwater like true sea animals, so they regularly visit the water's surface for air.

Whales are the most successful ocean colonizers. People often mistake them for fish. Whales **reproduce** in water and spend their entire lives there.

▼ Many birds are called sea birds, because they live on coastlines or on remote islands and rely on the oceans for their food. However, one bird in particular has mastered life in the oceans. The penguin spends most of its time swimming in cold waters, chasing fish and other sea animals.

▲ Animals are still turning to the world's oceans. Polar bears are considered to be marine mammals, because they spend most of their time on or in the frozen Arctic Ocean hunting seals. They are expert swimmers, and their wide, furry paws are webbed to help them move through the water.

▶ Sea reptiles, like turtles, are restricted to warm parts of the world's oceans. They leave the water to lay their eggs on sandy beaches.

OCEAN RESOURCES

People cannot live in the world's oceans, but they have always harvested the rich waters. As the human population has increased, people have turned to the oceans more and more for food and raw materials. Today more than 70 million tons (70 billion kilograms) of fish are caught each year, and one-fifth of the world's oil and gas is mined from the seabed.

Modern fishing methods are often so intensive that they devastate fish communities and upset the balance of ocean life. Many of yesterday's most fertile seas are no longer able to support large fishing fleets, because the fish stocks are so low.

The nets used by many of today's fishermen can also cause problems. They are made of nylon and do not rot underwater. If they are lost overboard, these nets become death traps to seals, dolphins, and other marine creatures that cannot detect them.

Fish are not the only animals people take from the ocean. Crabs and lobsters are two of our many seafood products. Sponges are chipped off the ocean floor and end up in bathrooms all over the world. Some seals and whales have been hunted to **extinction** for their meat, fur, and oil.

▼ Fishing is big business. Every day thousands of boats drag nets through the oceans to catch fish and other sea animals. This North Sea trawler is small compared to the largest fishing vessels. The world's supertrawlers can be more than 295 feet (90 meters) long.

OCEAN PRODUCTS

● Fish oils are used to make glue, soap, and margarine.

● A rare gem called a pearl is formed inside the shells of certain oysters.

● Big chunks of iron, copper, and manganese are lifted from the seabed using special suction pumps or are raked into nets by machines.

● In dry lands, seawater is sometimes treated to create a fresh water supply.

● Seaweed can be eaten as a vegetable and is also used to help make ice cream, toothpaste, paint, medicine, and other everyday products.

MAKING THE SEA SICK

Although we rely on the oceans for food, they are often treated like big garbage cans and sewers. Waste is pumped and dumped into the water, and **pesticides** and other human-made **pollutants** are washed into the ocean by rivers and streams.

The pollution of the world's oceans is harmful. Many sea animals are injured, strangled, or suffocated each year because of floating debris called flotsam. The high level of **toxic** wastes in a few seas is poisoning some animals and driving others away.

Land-locked seas like the Mediterranean are among the most polluted, but coastal waters everywhere are affected by the waste.

▶ Busy seaports can become virtual deserts of the ocean world. The oil, sewage, and litter spilled into the water make a harbor unfit for sea life.

▲ Oil spills threaten marine life. This poor sea bird will probably die unless the oil is cleaned from its feathers.

POLLUTION PROBLEMS

● Sealed barrels of dangerous radioactive and chemical waste have been dumped in some oceans, but no one knows if the containers are safe in the watery conditions.

● In some places around the world the local seafood is unfit to eat.

SAVING THE OCEANS

Countries around the world are beginning to realize the importance of the oceans. International laws have been made to restrict the amount of waste put into the water, and some marine mammals are now protected. Countries on the shores of the dirtiest seas have started major clean-up programs.

There is still a lot to be done. We need to understand patterns of marine life if we are to avoid overfishing and preserve future fish stocks. In recent years, enormous damage has been caused in some oceans by oil tankers spilling their deadly cargo. Oil blocks out light from the ocean, upsetting plankton production and so affecting all marine life. Through public pressure, oil companies could be persuaded to buy safer boats that would not leak in an accident.

Seemingly harmless activities in the oceans have now been found to have damaging effects on marine life. The electric cables that criss-cross the ocean floor disturb some seabed creatures and confuse many fish. Sharks bite into the cables, mistaking them for prey. The noise from boats, busy coastal resorts, and ocean-based industries frighten away seals, dolphins, and other animals from their traditional breeding grounds.

Whales have become a strong international symbol of ocean conservation. These extraordinary creatures have lived in the oceans far longer than people have lived on land. They are giants of the natural world.

Whales have been hunted for their oils and meat for so long that they are now difficult to find.

Most people agree that we must not kill any more whales, and laws have been made to protect the largest species. A few countries, however, continue to hunt whales and eat their meat as an expensive delicacy.

DAKUWACA FIGHTS FOR HIS LIFE

For thousands of years people have told stories about the world around them. Often these stories try to explain something that people do not really understand, like how the world began or where light comes from. This tale is told by the people of Fiji, who depend on the ocean that surrounds them for food and transportation.

Long ago the sharks were the rulers of the islands that make up Fiji in the Pacific Ocean. Each island had its own particular shark who lived beside the reef entrance of the island. These sharks patrolled the waters of their territory, challenging anyone who dared to come near. They allowed friends in but fought with hostile sharks until they paid a tribute.

Dakuwaca thought himself the greatest of all the sharks. He was big and fierce and enjoyed nothing better than a fight with another shark. He had never lost a fight, and he was quite sure he never would. He cared nothing for the terrible storms that his fights caused, whipping up the waters so that the islanders were tossed about in their boats. Often island houses were swept away by massive waves from the ocean.

Dakuwaca was patrolling his reef one day when he came across a shark named Masilaca. Masilaca was the mischief maker among the sharks. He did not fight much himself, but, with his wily ways, he had caused more fights than most sharks had fought!

"Good day, Dakuwaca," he said. "I suppose you're off for another fight. It's amazing the way you always beat the other sharks. I wish I were as good a fighter as you."

"No other shark is as good a fighter as I am," said Dakuwaca. "Hardly anyone bothers to challenge me any more. They all know that I am so much stronger than them. In fact it's getting very dull around here."

"Perhaps if you want a really good fight, you should go over to Kandavu Island. I hear there's a creature well worth fighting there, a mighty monster who guards the reef so that it is impossible to go near it. But no one ever goes there, because they are much too afraid of the creature," said Masilaca, with a sly glint in his eye. "Of course, I'm not suggesting that you're frightened. You're much too brave and strong. And I'm sure none of the other sharks think that you're afraid either."

Dakuwaca thrashed his tail through the water. Of course he wasn't afraid—what a suggestion! But if the other sharks thought he was afraid, he had better do something at once. Almost before Masilaca had finished speaking, Dakuwaca set off toward Kandavu, determined to challenge the fearsome monster.

As Dakuwaca approached Kandavu, he heard a deep, powerful voice calling from the shore. Dakuwaca had never heard anything like it before, and he found himself trembling a little.

"How foolish," he told himself. "Nothing on the shore can harm me." And he swam on.

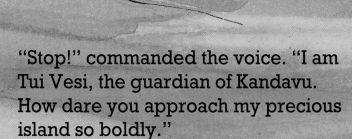

"Stop!" commanded the voice. "I am Tui Vesi, the guardian of Kandavu. How dare you approach my precious island so boldly."

Dakuwaca was rather frightened but determined not to show it.

"And I am Dakuwaca, the greatest of all sharks. Come out and fight to defend your island."

"I am a land guardian and so cannot come into the water to fight you," said Tui Vesi. "I shall send one of my servants to fight you instead. But be warned! It is a great and terrible monster, and it would be much better if you left now."

"No one is braver or stronger than I," said Dakuwaca. "I am not afraid of anything. I will fight your servant."

He swam around the mouth of the reef, watching and waiting for his opponent. His body was strong and quick, and his teeth were sharp.

Suddenly a giant arm appeared from the reef and grabbed him. A giant octopus! This wasn't what Dakuwaca was expecting at all! He thrashed and twisted to rid himself of the arm. His sharp teeth were quite useless, because he could not bend his body to bite at the arm. The arm loosened as he twisted, and for a moment Dakuwaca thought he was free. But no, two more arms whipped around, so that he could no longer move at all. And the arms began to squeeze tighter and tighter until Dakuwaca could bear it no longer.

"Have mercy!" he gasped. "Forgive my terrible presumption, Tui Vesi."

The arms of the octopus loosened slightly, and Tui Vesi's mighty voice boomed out into the waters once more.

"I will release you, Dakuwaca, providing that you promise to guard the people of my island from sharks that might attack them when they go out in their canoes."

"Yes, yes! Of course I will," Dakuwaca agreed.

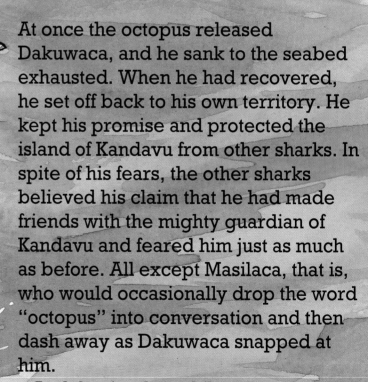

At once the octopus released Dakuwaca, and he sank to the seabed exhausted. When he had recovered, he set off back to his own territory. He kept his promise and protected the island of Kandavu from other sharks. In spite of his fears, the other sharks believed his claim that he had made friends with the mighty guardian of Kandavu and feared him just as much as before. All except Masilaca, that is, who would occasionally drop the word "octopus" into conversation and then dash away as Dakuwaca snapped at him.

And that is why, while other fishermen of the Fiji islands fear for their lives because of the sharks, the men of Kandavu ride happily in their canoes.

TRUE OR FALSE?

Which of these facts are true and which ones are false? If you have read this book carefully, you will know the answers.

1. Almost one-third of the world's surface is covered by oceans.

2. Dolphins and whales can stay underwater for several hours.

3. Sound travels through water five times faster than through air.

4. The world's four oceans are the Pacific, the Atlantic, the Mediterranean, and the Aegean.

5. It takes 5,000 years for one drop of seawater to travel through all the world's oceans.

6. Tsunamis are caused by underwater volcanic eruptions and earthquakes.

7. Plankton is a rich mixture made up of debris from seaweed.

8. Blue whales are the largest animals in the world.

9. Octopuses have 12 arms and feed mainly on seals.

10. Sharks must keep moving all the time or they will sink.

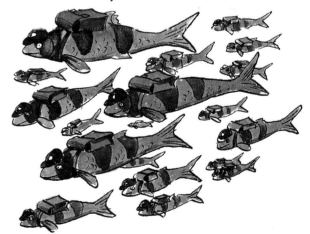

11. Fish travel in schools until they have learned how to protect themselves.

12. The paws of a polar bear are webbed.

13. Seaweed is used to help make ice cream.

Woodlands

LOOKING AT WOODLANDS

Woodlands are rich in animal and plant life. It is mainly the trees that keep the forest alive by providing food and **habitats** for wildlife.

There are many kinds of woodland, which are usually named after the types of trees that grow there. **Deciduous forests** have broadleaved trees such as oak, maple, and beech. They lose their leaves in winter and change color with the seasons.

Coniferous forests have **evergreen** trees such as pines and firs. These trees have needle-shaped leaves, which stay on the branches all year around. **Mixed woodlands** contain both coniferous and deciduous trees.

Temperate **rain forests** are warm and damp, but less so than tropical rain forests. They are very rich in unusual **species**, including the giant redwood trees of North America.

A TREE'S LIFE STORY

We can tell the age of a tree by the number of growth rings it has. Most trees grow a new layer of wood each year. Each layer makes another ring, which we can see when a tree is cut through. Some ancient bristlecone pines in North America have nearly 5,000 rings. The rings record hot, cold, and wet weather; pollution; and disease. Scientists can use them to learn about the climate and conditions of ancient times.

WHERE IN THE WORLD?

Because most land is found in the northern half of the world, most woodlands and forests are found here too. They lie between the cold Arctic and the hot, humid tropics. A band of coniferous forests runs across the north from Alaska to Siberia. Deciduous forests grow throughout North America, Europe, and Asia. Mixed woodlands grow in some of these areas, too. There are pockets of temperate rain forest in The United States, China, Japan, and New Zealand. Tropical rain forests grow near the Equator.

▶ In deciduous forests, the leaves on the trees lose their green color, dry out, and fall in autumn.

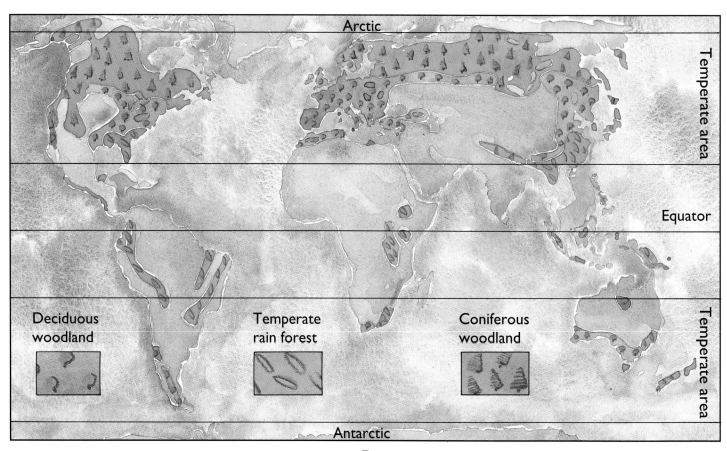

Arctic

Temperate area

Equator

Temperate area

Antarctic

Deciduous woodland

Temperate rain forest

Coniferous woodland

▲ The mountains in Colorado have mixed woodlands. Deciduous trees show their bright autumn colors, while snow covers the coniferous trees.

◀ Temperate rain forests have some of the world's tallest trees. Black bears, black-tailed deer, and the tiniest moles also live there.

Until a few hundred years ago, most of Europe and North America was covered with forest. People say that a squirrel could have crossed a whole **continent** without touching the ground. Today, only a fraction of that woodland is left. Much disappeared to make way for farming and building. The original **wildwoods** are now rare, although areas do still exist, for example in Poland, France, Great Britain, and North America.

SEASONAL CYCLES

Life in a woodland is always changing. In early spring, the days grow longer and warmer. **Migrating** birds arrive and build their nests. Flowers appear on the woodland floor. The first of the baby animals are born. They feed on the new green leaves so that they can grow strong before the cold weather comes. Sometimes animals have a second family to make sure that some young survive. When the summer comes, the forest buzzes with activity. Insects hatch, and woodland creatures feast on the nuts and fruits growing around them.

▲ The forest floor sometimes looks bare, because leaves and branches block out the light. Few plants can survive in the dark, shady area below.

◄ Most woodland flowers, such as these bluebells and red campions, bloom in late spring and early summer. They have to make the most of the sunlight to help them grow before the leaves on the trees open fully and cast a shadow over them. The range of species of flowers growing in an area of woodland can tell us about its age. Older woodlands often have a much wider variety than younger ones, and there are some species that can be found only in ancient woodlands.

◀ Woodland creatures such as hedgehogs, dormice, and woodchucks hibernate through the winter. They curl up into a tight ball and stay fast asleep. Their bodies cool down to save energy. Squirrels, bears, and badgers doze during the cold months, waking and moving around from time to time. Squirrels nibble nuts they stored in the autumn.

▼ The coats of some deer species change color with the seasons. This helps them to hide from **predators** when the landscape around them changes. An ermine's coat also changes, from brown in the summer to white in the winter.

Gradually the days grow shorter and colder. Trees prepare for the winter, changing color and then shedding their leaves. Animals grow thick coats and gather food that must last until spring. Some animals **hibernate** to escape the cold. Many species of birds migrate to warmer lands. Snow covers young plants like a blanket to protect them from frost. In the spring, the cycle begins again.

LEAF LIFE

Trees are a source of life for all the plants and animals in a woodland. They are **ecosystems** in themselves. The oak tree alone offers food and shelter to more than 300 species of insects. Most woodland trees grow from nuts that are spread by animals or, like other woodland plants, from seeds carried by the wind. This is why woodland flowers such as forget-me-nots are so small and hidden. They do not need to attract insects or birds to help them reproduce.

▶ American leaf-cutter ants take pieces of leaves into their nests. They use the leaves to fertilize the tiny fungus on which they feed.

LIFE IN A LOG

Nothing is wasted in a woodland. A fallen log lying on the forest floor gives food to other living things and is soon humming with new life. First the slugs and woodlice arrive. They are eaten by centipedes and spiders. A year or so later, fungi, mosses, and flowers coat the bark. Beetles chew into the wood, and reptiles such as lizards and snakes lie in wait for them. By the following year, hundreds of insects are busy laying eggs and storing food. Birds come to feed on them. Finally, the insects help the log to crumble, and it becomes part of the soil and helps new trees and other plants to grow.

Each species of tree grows best in a particular kind of soil and climate. Ancient oaks are at home in western Europe, as are beeches. These also grow in North America, along with giant redwoods and maples. In Russia and Canada, pines, larches, and other coniferous trees make up the biggest forests in the world. Massive kauri trees are native to New Zealand, where Maori people once made war canoes from them.

▲ The needles on a pine tree help it during the winter. When the ground is frozen, water cannot reach the trunk through the roots. Instead, the needles have a coating of wax that keeps the water inside them from escaping. The shape of the needles makes it difficult for snow to settle on the branches. Their dark color also helps them to absorb extra warmth from the sun.

▲ Many forest trees produce fruits and berries. These make a good meal for insects and birds such as the cedar waxwing of North America. People also eat some woodland fruits and can make use of every part of a tree, even the bark. Oak bark is sometimes used as a medicine for sore throats and nosebleeds, while witch hazel bark and leaves can soothe cuts and bruises.

FOREST BIRDS

Each woodland bird has its favorite niche or place in the forest. Eagles and hawks keep a lookout high in the branches. Owls and nuthatches peer out of old tree holes, and capercaillie rummage about on the forest floor. In spring, the forest hums with birdsongs from dawn to dusk. This is how birds claim their **territory** and attract a mate. Some give their mates a special **courtship display**. Waxwings give each other "presents," while male scarlet tanagers have bright, eye-catching red feathers.

Adult birds are always busy. They need to feed their chicks every few hours. Some have adapted especially to forest foods. Crossbills hook pine nuts out of cones with their unusual crossed-over beaks. Nutcrackers wedge nuts in crevices and drill out the kernel. They store nuts for the winter but sometimes forget where they left them. Woodpeckers eat ants in summer and pine nuts in winter. Nuthatches can hang upside down on tree trunks to catch insects. Sapsuckers trap insects in tree sap.

WINTER HOLIDAYS

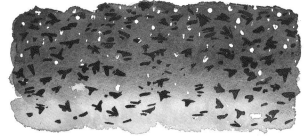

Some birds migrate to escape the cold winter. Warblers steer by the stars to find their way, while thrushes follow the sun. Young cuckoos fly all the way to Africa without their parents. They all fly back again the following spring to build their nests.

◀ Woodpeckers use their beaks as high-speed drills to make holes in trees for nesting or hunting for food. They have very long, sticky tongues that they keep curled up inside their heads. When they have made a hole in the bark or wood of a tree, they reach their tongues inside and pick up insects.

▼ Tawny owls feed on mice and voles, which they catch from the forest floor and surrounding countryside. But they are under threat. Their woodland habitat has been destroyed in many places, forcing them to hunt in towns and near busy roads.

FOREST VEGETARIANS

Trees provide a larder for thousands of forest creatures. Insect **larvae** burrow into wood. Caterpillars chew leaf edges. Plant bugs suck tree sap. Deer, moose, rabbits, and hares munch new green shoots. In winter they eat nuts, berries, and bark, as do squirrels and wild boar. Worms and mites working deep in the forest floor transform dead leaves, which fall in the autumn, into new soil for the following spring.

▶ Beavers are expert engineers. They cut down whole trees with their sharp teeth to build dams and lodges in which to live. These homes have an underwater entrance to keep predators from getting in. Each part of the dam and lodge is built so that there will be no flooding.

FIGHTING FACTS

● When in danger, a squirrel can stay quite still for half an hour. It warns its family by thumping its feet and slapping its tail on the ground. If it is in a tree when an enemy is near, it drops down to a safe lower branch.

● Male deer fight "duels" in the breeding season. They use their antlers as weapons. The strongest one wins a whole herd of female deer with which to mate.

▶ Moose feed on leaves, tree shoots, twigs, and grasses. They have very soft, pliable lips and long muzzles that they use to delicately pick juicy leaves from high branches. They often bend young trees by pushing against the trunks as they reach up for the tender leaves growing at the top. They also eat plants from the bottom of forest lakes and prefer to live in swampy woodland areas.

▼ Chipmunks belong to the same family as squirrels. They burrow underground and build their nests in tunnels. Here they store food such as seeds and nuts that will last through their winter hibernation.

Many plant-eating woodland insects are very secretive in order to avoid predators. The female sawfly hides her eggs in pine needles. She slices the needles open with special "saws" on her legs and lays her eggs inside. Weevils roll up leaves into tubes and hide their eggs inside. Other insects disguise themselves to look like buds, bird droppings, twigs, or dead leaves to fool their enemies.

FOREST HUNTERS

Big forest **carnivores** are becoming rare. There are more of them in the coniferous forests of the north, because they are farther from the people who affect their woodland environment. Bears and wolves have suffered badly from the loss of large areas of forest, which have been cleared to make room for new buildings or farmland.

Lynx and wildcats sit high in the trees ready to pounce on small **rodents**. Wolves hunt together in packs for caribou, moose, and deer. They waste nothing and may bury leftovers for another day.

▼ Like badgers, wolves, and bats, foxes usually wait until dark to venture out of their dens to hunt. When cubs are a few weeks old, their mother takes them out for hunting lessons.

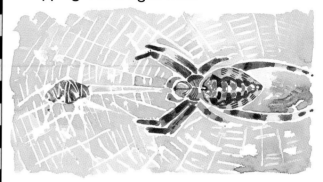

▲ Northern European forest dwellers such as the Lapp people herd reindeer as part of their traditional way of life. But now some of the forests where they spend the winter are threatened by logging companies.

◄ Bears love to eat fish. They wait in streams for salmon to leap out of the water. They also climb trees to raid insect nests in search of honey.

There were once many groups of **nomadic** forest people, such as **Native** Americans who hunted moose, deer, and beaver. A few still live as their ancestors did, but many were driven out by European settlers. The forests where they used to live are now being destroyed by developers who plan to exploit their **resources**.

WOODLAND RESOURCES

We all depend on the forest. In the north of the world, we use wood to make our lives comfortable. Many things that we use every day, from tables and chairs to pianos and guitars, begin as a tree. We turn wood into paper, then into books, newspapers, and packaging. Some of us use as many as 100 sheets of paper in a day. In the south of the world, wood is essential to survival. Half of all the trees cut down are used for fuel.

All sorts of fruits, nuts, seeds, and spices come from the world's forests.

Chestnuts and hazelnuts grow in deciduous woodlands. Apple, apricot, peach, and plum trees are traditional woodland species. Today, they are cultivated, and the fruits are sold fresh or dry. The sap from maple trees makes maple syrup.

However, even with all these products, we take very little food from the forest compared to the quantity of wood we use.

▼ This Gambian woman carries home a supply of wood, which she will burn to provide heat, cook food, and heat water.

CORK FACTS

Cork comes from the bark of the cork oak tree. It is stripped off only once every 10 years to allow the tree to grow a new layer. When the bark is dry it is processed to make floor tiles and corks for bottles.

▲ Paper comes from coniferous trees like the spruce, pine, and larch. Millions of these trees are cut down every year. The wood is chopped up, pulped, mixed with water, and spread out to dry. It is then used to make newsprint, books, packaging, and other paper products.

▲ The simple pine tree gives us pine nuts, paper, glue, and perfumes.

In addition to being an important resource for people, woodlands house millions of unique plants and animals. They also hold soil in place so it does not wash away. They provide moisture for rain, and they help to keep our climate in balance.

SHRINKING WOODLANDS

It is not just tropical rain forests that are disappearing today. Ancient woodlands are going too. In Canada, two-thirds of the forests have already vanished. In North America, only 1 tree in every 20 is spared.

Half of Britain's wildwoods have disappeared in the last century. Beavers, bears, and lynx went with them. In Scandinavia, many of the

newly planted forests contain only one tree species.

Trees are cut down to make way for homes, farming, and industry. Some are destroyed by forest fires, others by storms. "Acid rain" caused by factory fumes kills trees and pollutes the soil, rivers, and lakes. Germany's white fir trees have been damaged in this way. Hunting, too, endangers animals. For example, there are very few bison left living wild in the world today.

The results are serious. Rare plants and animals are losing their habitats. Soil is **eroding**, climate patterns are changing, and droughts and floods are increasing as the world gradually heats up. We need to act now. Our future depends on it.

DID YOU KNOW?

● When logging companies cut down trees in North America, a quarter of them are not used and are left on the ground to rot.

● Since 1950, over half the world's trees have disappeared, and many species are now under threat.

● We are losing 68 species of wildlife every day. Not since the time of the dinosaurs have so many unique species disappeared every day.

SAVING OUR WOODLANDS

All over the world, people are working to protect woodlands and their wildlife. Environmental groups are campaigning to save endangered species. The sable used to be killed for its hair, which was used to make paintbrushes. Happily, it has been saved from **extinction**. National Parks in many places allow animals to live and breed in peace. People are not allowed to hunt or light fires in these areas.

We need to take even better care of our woodlands. In Sweden and Finland, more trees are planted than cut down. But only one or two species are planted, so the wildlife is suffering. It needs a variety of trees to make up its true habitat. If we doubled the amount of paper we recycle, we could reduce by half the number of trees we cut down. This would help to preserve the rich, ancient forests that remain. Governments need to take urgent action to reduce pollution and prevent further **deforestation** and loss of species. They could also encourage **conservation**.

▲ Some Hindus in parts of India hold special ceremonies in which they offer gifts to trees to show their respect for nature and living things.

◀ Tree-planting programs are being set up in every country. These children in Sri Lanka are taking seedlings to a tree nursery to plant.

The Chipko Movement was started by a group of Indian women who saved their forest from loggers by hugging the trees. When the axemen came, the women surrounded the trunks and refused to move. They explained how the trees prevent the soil from eroding and help to keep the rivers flowing. The government agreed to stop the logging.

WHAT YOU CAN DO

● Join a conservation group. Support its work, find out more, and even help to protect a rare bird or animal.

● Collect a few acorns and conkers in the autumn. Plant them in your yard, at school, or in a patch of wasteland. Take care of them and watch them grow.

● Start a paper-recycling or tree-planting program at school or where you live.

● Encourage your family to buy environment-friendly and recycled products.

BOMBO MEETS MOTHER EAGLE

For thousands of years people have told stories about the world around them. Often these stories try to explain something that people do not understand. This tale is told by the Iroquois people of the forests of the Eastern United States.

Bombo was a great hunter. He lived deep in the forests of Pennsylvania and caught more deer than any hunter his people had ever known. Every morning he set out with his special green bow and his long, sharp arrows. Every lunchtime he returned with a deer slung over his shoulder.

Bombo had magic power. All he had to do was call to the deer, and they would come and graze near his home. But he was not satisfied. He wanted more.

One day he decided to test his power. He called to the eagles, "Hey, Eagles, I have fresh meat here for you. Come and take it to your aeries." Golden eagles swooped down from all directions. There were males, females, and even some young ones who had only just learned to fly. But as they reached the feast, Bombo shot them one by one and stole their feathers.

The next day, Bombo called the eagles again. Eighteen female birds glided majestically down to find food for their chicks. He aimed his arrow and was just about to shoot when a voice behind him said, "Stop!" Bombo swung around in surprise. Standing before him was his best friend, Lilo.

"This is very dangerous, Bombo," he warned. "You must stop immediately. The animals are upset and angry. It is wrong to shoot the eagles and take their feathers."

"Nonsense," replied Bombo. "I'm not doing any harm. Look at my beautiful feather collection. I can make some amazing arrows now."

"You're wrong," said Lilo. "I'm your friend, and I don't want to see you hurt, but if you don't stop, the animals will teach you a lesson."

But Bombo ignored his friend and walked off, shaking his head.

The next day Bombo called the eagles for the third time. To his surprise, nothing happened. The forest remained silent and still. As Bombo strained his ears for some sound from the eagles, he thought that he could hear a faint humming. Suddenly, a gigantic dark shape loomed out of the sky toward him. It was the mother of all eagles – and she was very, very angry. Bombo had never been so terrified in his life. He took one look at her and ran off as fast as he could. He spotted a hollow log and quickly wriggled inside, but Mother Eagle was just behind him. She grabbed him with her huge claws and swept him up into the air with two angry beats of her powerful wings.

They flew up and up until the forest looked like a green carpet below them. Bombo's heart was beating faster and faster. He felt dizzy. The forest seemed to turn from green to blue. Mother Eagle swooped up and down and around in circles until Bombo thought he would die. As they soared up again, he thought he glimpsed the edge of the forest way below. He panicked. Were they about to leave his home altogether?

All of a sudden, they were heading straight for a huge tree. Just as Bombo was sure they were going to crash, Mother Eagle swooped down into her aerie, dropped him into her nest with her chicks, and flew off.

Bombo was terrified. How would he get home now? Suddenly he had an idea. In his pocket he had some dried meat and leather thongs. He offered the meat to the eaglets, who gobbled it up greedily, then he tied their beaks with the thongs.

When Mother Eagle came back with food for her chicks and saw what Bombo had done, she was furious.

"This is wrong, Bombo. Untie them this minute," she cried.

"No," replied Bombo. "I won't untie them until you promise to let me go."

For two days Mother Eagle tried to unpick the tight leather thongs with her sharp beak, but to no avail. Meanwhile, her chicks grew thinner and thinner. They were soon so weak that they could hardly stand up. Mother Eagle flew off around the forest with a grave look on her face.

Finally, she returned to the nest.

"I'll make a pact with you, Bombo," she said. "If you promise never to kill another eagle without permission from the Spirit World, and if you untie my chicks this minute, you may safely go back to your home."

"I promise," he replied, untying the thongs so that the hungry chicks could eat at last. As Mother Eagle fed her family, Bombo saw them grow big and strong right before his eyes. Suddenly, before he could even blink, he found himself back, safe and sound, in his own home.

From that day on, whenever Bombo caught a deer, he called the eagles and invited them to come and share the meal in safety. He never killed another eagle, and the only feathers he collected were the ones the eagles left for him. From then on, all the hunters in the forest followed Bombo's example. The eagles and the forest people understood one another at last.

TRUE OR FALSE?

Which of these facts are true and which ones are false?
If you have read this book carefully, you will know the answers.

1. Most woodlands are in the top half of the world.

2. Beavers warn their families of trouble by thumping their feet and slapping their tails.

3. Ermines have a white coat in summer and a brown coat in winter.

4. Nuthatches stand upside down on tree trunks to catch insects.

5. A woodpecker has such a long tongue that it has to keep it curled up inside its head.

6. Waxwings have bright red feathers to attract a mate.

7. If a wolf is attacked, its tail can drop off to allow it to escape.

8. Indian women saved their forest by hugging the trees.

9. Rabbits have special skin flaps so that they can fly through the forest.

10. Maori people used pine trees to make war canoes.

Rain Forests

LOOKING AT RAIN FORESTS

Imagine a forest unchanged for 60 million years, where giant trees reach up to the sky, their leafy branches blocking out light to the forest floor below. Imagine a place where the temperature hardly changes from day to night, season to season, year to year. A place where rain clouds hang in the air and heavy downpours are common. The rain forest is such a place.

About half the world's species of plants and animals live in rain forests. More species of animals live in rain forests than anywhere else in the world.

Rain forests are home not only to large numbers of animals and plants. People have lived in rain forests for generations.

DID YOU KNOW?

● Rain forests are the wettest areas of land in the world. More than 32 feet (10 meters) of rain may fall during a single year in some places.

● Almost half of the world's rain forests have been cut down in the last 50 years and the clearance continues. In 1989 rain forests were disappearing at a rate of 60 acres (24 hectares) every minute.

LAYERS OF THE RAIN FOREST

Most rain forest life is found about 120 feet (40 meters) above the ground, in the **canopy**. This is where the branches of the giant trees tangle together to form a lush, green platform.

Underneath the canopy, little can grow in the darkness. Where light does get through the canopy, smaller trees and plants compete for space.

Little grows on the forest floor, but leaves and other debris rain down from the canopy. Plants, insects, and animals change this waste into food

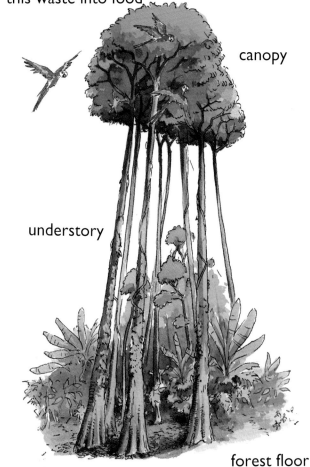

canopy

understory

forest floor

WHERE IN THE WORLD?

More than half of the world's rain forests are in South and Central America. The remainder can be found in parts of Africa, Asia, and Australia. Almost all rain forests lie between two imaginary lines north and south of the **equator**, called the **Tropic of Cancer** and the **Tropic of Capricorn**. This is why they are often called tropical rain forests.

It has been hot and wet in the tropics for millions of years. These constant conditions have made it possible for rain forests to develop into the most diverse and complex **environments** in the world. Some scientists recognize more than 40 different types of rain forest, each with its own variety of plant and animal life.

Rain forests once formed a wide, green belt around the planet, but today pictures taken from space tell a different story. All around the world large areas of rain forest are vanishing as people clear the way for crops, homes, and businesses. Many species of wildlife are disappearing, too.

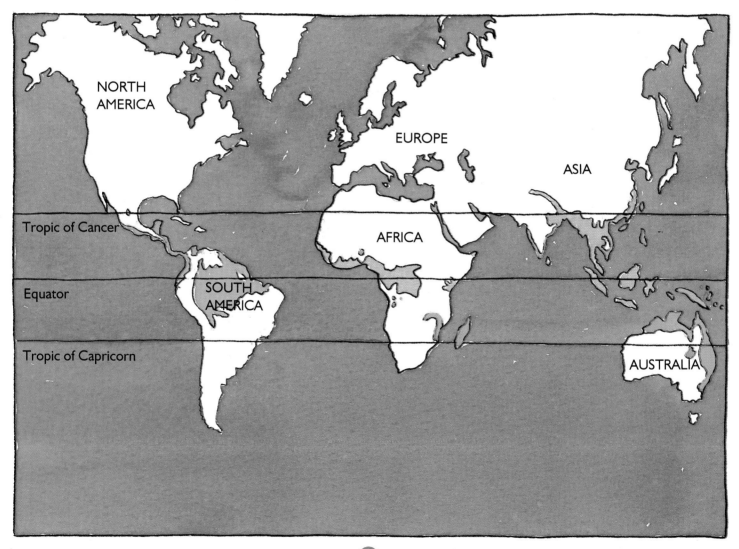

NORTH AMERICA

EUROPE

ASIA

Tropic of Cancer

AFRICA

Equator

SOUTH AMERICA

Tropic of Capricorn

AUSTRALIA

▶ In the tropics, the only change in weather conditions is from wet to wetter during the rainy season. This means that rain forest trees do not need to flower in spring or shed their leaves in autumn. Each type of tree has its own growth cycle. The varying tree cycles guarantee a regular supply of flowers, fruits, nuts, and seeds for rain forest creatures.

▼ The largest rain forest in the world stretches across the Amazon Basin in South America. It covers an area nearly as big as Australia. The Amazon River snakes through the rain forest. It is the largest river system in the world. During the rainy season, parts of the rain forest are flooded by the Amazon and fish swim among the giant tree trunks.

THE PLANT BANK

Most woodlands grow one type of tree such as oak or maple. In the rain forest of South America scientists have counted as many as 280 species in one 2½-acre (1-hectare) area.

Rain forests contain a huge variety of other plants, too. Wherever light reaches the forest floor, an exotic layer of herbs and ferns flourishes. Wiry stems hang like lifeless ropes around the giant tree trunks. These climbers and vines produce a mass of leaves and flowers in the canopy layer.

The canopy itself is like a huge aerial garden. Moss, lichen, and hundreds of flowering plants cover the canopy branches. These plants, called **epiphytes**, do not harm the host tree. Their roots dangle in the air or grow in a thin layer of compost, which forms in the dips and cracks of the many branches.

▲ The rafflesia grows on the forest floor in parts of Asia. It produces flowers up to 3 feet (1 meter) across—the biggest in the world. They have thick, warty petals and spiky centers that stink of rotting meat.

▶ Water and debris collect in some epiphytes and provide ponds for tiny rain forest frogs.

PLANT FACTS

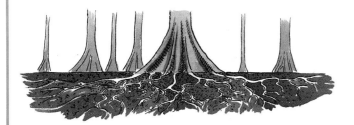

Rain forest trees have shallow root systems, so they often produce special **buttress roots** to help keep themselves standing upright.

Most rain forest leaves are thick and waxy with special **drip-tips** to drain away water. They are often so big they can be used as umbrellas.

FEASTING IN THE FOREST

The lush vegetation of the rain forest is home to millions of different insects and other creepy crawlies. Some, like flies and beetles, act as cleaners, clearing the forest floor of waste and debris. Others, like wasps and bees, help to pollinate the flowers of the forest. Ants and spiders are also in abundance. Between them, they eat large numbers of other insects and so keep them from becoming too plentiful.

The plants and insects of the rain forest provide thousands of different animals with food to eat. Shown here are some of the animals that can be found feasting in the forests.

▲ Lizards can be found all over the rain forest, eating insects, plants, and occasionally, small animals. Most lizards seize insects in their mouths, but a few snatch them from the air with their extra-long tongues.

◄ The giant, red orangutans have huge appetites. They love to eat fruit, but they will also chew leaves, shoots, and tree bark, and occasionally, they will take eggs from birds' nests. To help them find their favorite fruit, the clever orangutans watch the birds that share their tastes in food and follow them through the forest. Orangutans spend most of their lives in the treetops, swinging from branch to branch. Their long, powerful arms and hook-shaped hands make treetop climbing easy work. Orangutans can be found in the rain forests of Borneo and Sumatra in Southeast Asia.

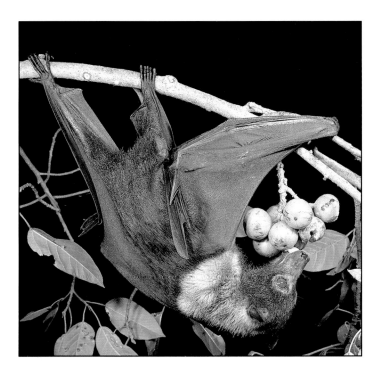

▲ Bats are commonplace in the rain forest. They are not birds but instead the world's only flying mammals. Many bats hunt insects, but some, like the flying fox shown here, eat fruit. Fruit bats help to spread seeds around the forest.

▲ The hummingbird's long, thin bill is ideal for getting to the sweet nectar found inside flowers. But these birds also eat insects. Hummingbirds are flying experts and can even fly backward.

▶ Sloths have strict leaf-eating diets. They spend practically all their time in the treetops. There are two-toed sloths and three-toed sloths, like the one in this picture. Algae, beetles, moths, and mites hide in the sloth's fur.

FOREST FIENDS

The rain forest is a dangerous place. The brightly colored parrots, chattering monkeys, and slumbering sloths may seem carefree, but they have their enemies. When a giant eagle soars overhead or an agile cat is on the prowl, the whole canopy is gripped in terror.

Big cats and eagles are the largest hunters in the forest, but there are hundreds of others. In the canopy, long, slender tree snakes catch lizards, frogs, and small birds. On the forest floor, huge, heavy constrictors, like the anaconda, wait for larger prey such as wild boar or deer that forage in the leaf litter.

Small creatures can pose a greater threat to life. Scorpions, spiders, bees, and wasps are found all over the forest. Many have poisonous bites or stings that can cause rashes, sickness, or even death.

▲ Each rain forest has its own type of giant eagle. In Africa it is the crowned eagle, in South America the harpy eagle, and in Asia the monkey-eating eagle, shown here. Giant eagles catch monkeys, sloths, and other large prey in the canopy layer.

◄ Some forest cats, such as the margay and clouded leopard, are excellent tree climbers. They will chase monkeys and squirrels through the understory. Others, like this jaguar, prefer to wait quietly on low, overhanging branches and pounce on animals as they pass beneath them.

◄ The bushmaster hunts small animals that **scavenge** on the forest floor. It is a venomous snake, which means that it injects poison when it bites. The bushmaster is one of the most feared snakes in South America. Its bite can kill a person within hours. Luckily this snake is shy and not often seen!

PROTECTION FROM PERIL

The smallest rain forest creatures have the greatest number of natural enemies, so it is not surprising that they have developed many ways to defend themselves.

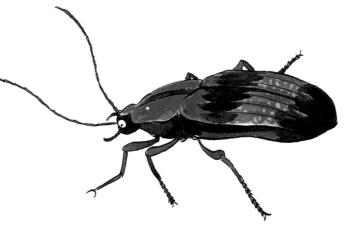

Some rain forest creatures produce a poison in their bodies that makes them unpleasant to eat. Bold markings advertise the fact, and predators learn to recognize these warning signals.

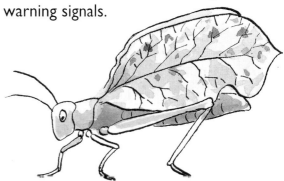

Some butterflies have hidden eyespots on their wings, which are flashed at would-be predators. The false eyes startle the attackers, and this gives the butterflies a chance to escape.

To reduce the risk of being eaten, many insects have clever **camouflage**, like this bush cricket.

RAIN FOREST PEOPLE

Modern people are uncomfortable in the rain forest. They find the hot, humid conditions stifling. Every step they take is fraught with danger, and although there is food all around them, they cannot tell a poisonous berry from a nutritious and refreshing fruit.

Certain groups of people have lived in the rain forests for thousands of years. To them, the rain forest is home and the only world they know. Rain forest **tribes** live in structured communities with their own cultures and customs. They have a deep understanding of the way the rain forest works. They know how to take from the forest without causing harm.

There are rain forest tribes in parts of Africa, Asia, and South America, but their way of life is threatened. Although they have rights according to international laws, they are often mistreated and their land is stolen or invaded. If all the ancient tribes disappear, their detailed knowledge of the rain forest may be lost forever.

▼ A large area of rain forest can support only a few hundred people, so rain forest tribes are spread thinly through the wooded lands. Some tribes build communal houses, where many families live together.

◀ Rain forest children do not have to go to school, but they still have a lot to learn. Their elders must teach them everything there is to know about life in the rain forest.

▼ Many rain forest peoples paint their bodies with colorful dyes and use feathers, flowers, and other natural materials to make simple pieces of jewelry.

PEOPLE FACTS

The Pygmy people of the African rain forest are very small. The tallest Pygmies are only 4 feet 8 inches (1.4 meters) tall.

Life is not easy in the rain forest. A person in the modern world may live for more than 70 years. In the rain forest, few people survive more than 40 years. Diseases like flu and measles, introduced by European settlers, are still big killers of native tribes. More than 80 different tribes have died out in Brazil since 1900.

GIFTS FROM THE FOREST

Rain forest tribes can get everything they need from their homeland. The many different plants and animals found in the forest provide raw materials for meals, houses, clothes, medicines, tools, and cosmetics.

We also use rain forest products. Many of the fruits, nuts, and cereals that fill our supermarket shelves originated in the rain forest. The domestic chicken, which is now farmed worldwide, began its life on the forest floor. The most expensive **hardwoods** such as teak, mahogany, and ebony come from rain forest trees.

Other rain forest products include tea, coffee, cocoa, rubber, and many types of medicine.

We still know very little about the rain forest. Scientists believe there are thousands of future foodstuffs, medicines, and other raw materials waiting there to be discovered.

▼ These tiny rain forest frogs produce a strong poison under their skin to stop other animals from eating them. Some tribes extract this poison by gently roasting the frogs and collecting their sweat. They use it on the tips of their blow-pipe darts when they hunt big game.

RAIN FOREST TREASURES

There is an Amazonian tree that produces a sap very similar to diesel fuel. It can be poured straight into a truck's tank and used as fuel.

One-fourth of all medicines came from rain forest plants and animals.

Rain forest insects could offer an alternative to expensive pesticides. In Florida, three kinds of wasp were successfully introduced to control pests that were damaging the citrus tree crops.

There are at least 1,500 potential new fruits and vegetables growing in the world's rain forests.

▲ A hunter from the Yanomami tribe hunts monkeys and other game, while women and children search the forest floor for food.

RAIN FOREST DESTRUCTION

Rain forests are natural treasure-houses, but they are being destroyed for nothing more than timber and the land on which they stand. This is because most rain forests are found in poor, developing countries. These countries cannot afford to keep their beautiful forests.

Large areas of rain forest are sold to timber companies. They send bulldozers and chainsaw gangs into the forest to cut down the hardwood trees. The wildlife flees and, although only the oldest and largest trees are felled, over half of the forest may be damaged by the time all the work is finished.

▼ An estimated 500 million people have moved into the world's rain forests, and more are sure to follow. They clear the forest to farm small areas of land for food and money.

Rain forests are cleared completely to reach rich mineral reserves, such as iron, copper, or uranium, or to make huge cash-crop plantations of coffee, cocoa, or bananas.

Big business is only half the story. There are thousands of poor, homeless people in rain forest countries who are encouraged to leave the overcrowded cities and farm pieces of rain forest land. They are called **slash-and-burn farmers**, because they build simple homesteads in the forest and then burn the surrounding vegetation to enrich the soil.

DID YOU KNOW?

● Industrial countries buy more than 18 times more hardwood today than they did 50 years ago.

● Over half of Central America's rain forests are gone. They have been cleared to build huge cattle ranches. Much of the meat produced is sold to western countries to feed the demands of their growing burger market.

▶ See the difference between the rich world of the distant green rain forest and the lifeless cracked earth in the foreground? Huge areas of Brazil have been devastated, and animals and plants are gone forever.

PARADISE LOST

It can take less than 10 years for rain forest land to become as barren and lifeless as a desert. This is because most rain forests are found on poor clay soils. Only a thin layer of nutritious **topsoil** covers the forest floor, and this is anchored by giant tree trunks.

Slash-and-burn farmers clear rain forest land to grow their crops. But after only a few years, the tropical rains wash the topsoil away, and the land becomes too difficult to cultivate.

FROM GOOD TO BAD

Trees and plants help to keep the air around us clean. They use sunlight, water, and air to make food. In the food-making process, they make use of the part of the air that we breathe out (carbon dioxide) and produce the part that we breathe in (oxygen).

When rain forests are burned down to clear land, the trees stop using up carbon dioxide. Instead, the forest fires produce carbon dioxide, which pollutes the atmosphere.

The wastelands left behind by farmers are baked by the sun and drenched by rain. The rain, which would have watered thirsty trees and plants, falls straight to the ground and runs downhill, carrying tons of soil with it. Valleys are flooded, and freshwater rivers become clogged with mud.

Tropical scientists believe that, at the present rate of destruction, there will be no rain forests left by the year 2050. If this paradise is lost, thousands of different plants and animals will disappear forever.

SAVING THE FORESTS

More and more people are becoming aware of the need to save the rain forests. Some steps have already been taken to slow the rate of destruction. Native tribes have blocked the path of bulldozers and chainsaw gangs, and many **conservation** groups have launched huge rain forest campaigns.

Much more could still be done to save the world's rain forests. Timber companies could change the way they harvest the forest to reduce the amount of damage they cause. They could also be forced to replant areas of forest that have been disturbed. Slash-and-burn farmers could be taught better ways to farm rain forest lands. By planting trees and crops together, they could preserve the fragile topsoil and use the same piece of land for many years.

Rich, industrial countries could help, too. Rain forest countries are using up their beautiful forests to pay off huge debts to western countries. If these debts were reduced, more money could be spent on developing the cleared land, and the remaining forests could be preserved.

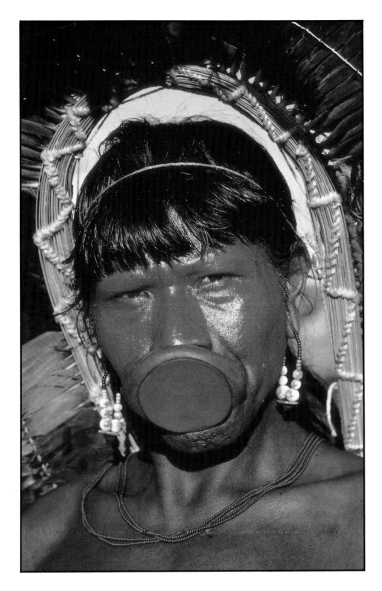

▲ Raoni is a chief of the Kayapo Indians in Brazil. He has traveled many miles (kilometers) from his rain forest home to speak about the problems his people face. Their land has been invaded by foresters and slash-and-burn farmers. The forests, which they rely upon for food and shelter, are being destroyed.

◀ Scientists believe that more than 50 wild species of insects, plants, and animals become **extinct** every day because of rain forest destruction. Many of the world's favorite animals such as tigers and orangutans are endangered because their rain forest homes are being destroyed. By protecting large areas of rain forest, these animals could be saved from extinction.

RAIN FOREST ACTION

Spread the Word
Tell your friends and relatives about the plight of the rain forests. Write to your congresspeople and ask them to help rain forest countries.

Support Rain Forest Campaigns
There are many charities and pressure groups trying to slow the rate of rain forest destruction. They need money and support to continue their work. Watch for news on television, on the radio, or in newspapers and magazines of how you can help them.

THE COWRIE THIEVES

For thousands of years people have told stories about the world around them. Often these stories try to explain something that people do not really understand, like how the world began or where light comes from. This tale is told by the people of the Congo in Africa.

Long ago, in a village right in the middle of the Congo, there lived a man and his wife who were always causing mischief.

All the other villagers agreed that these two had the most irritating habits. They hardly ever did any work, preferring to sit around and chatter to one another. When they did start to work, they would tire of whatever they were doing very quickly and wander off to do something else.

They were always dropping in at their neighbors' huts, just when dinner was ready. Their neighbors were obliged to ask them in to supper; that being the custom.

But the worst thing of all was the way they would pick up other people's belongings. The two of them would just wander into other people's huts and start picking up anything that they could see. They would poke their noses into baskets, take a mouthful of food, or just move everything around so that the owner of the hut would come home to a terrible mess.

The other villagers put up with the pair because they never really did much harm. Whenever a villager lost his temper with them, they looked so hurt at the thought that they had done wrong and promised so fervently to mend their ways. It was impossible to be angry with them for long.

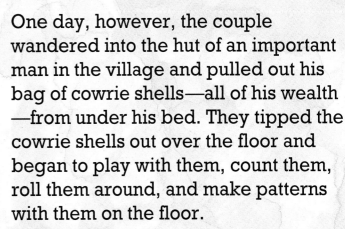

One day, however, the couple wandered into the hut of an important man in the village and pulled out his bag of cowrie shells—all of his wealth—from under his bed. They tipped the cowrie shells out over the floor and began to play with them, count them, roll them around, and make patterns with them on the floor.

Eventually the mischievous man decided to go find some food, and his mischievous wife followed him, leaving the cowrie shells scattered all over the floor.

When the owner of the hut came back and saw his cowrie shells scattered about, his first thought was that he had been robbed.

He shouted to all the other villagers to come and see what had happened. The woman from the hut next door said that she had seen the mischievous man and his mischievous wife coming out of the important man's hut.

Just then, someone spotted the mischievous man and his mischievous wife coming around the corner with a bunch of bananas. They looked very surprised when they were accused of stealing the cowrie shells.

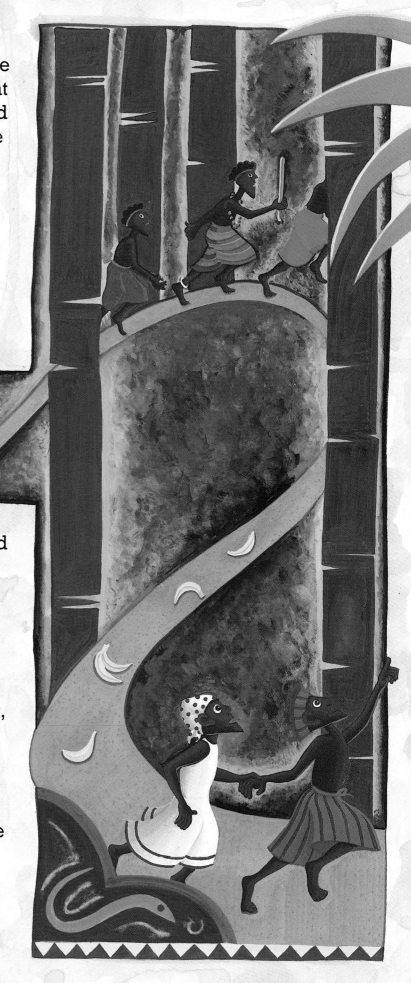

The important man who thought he had been robbed did not wait for an explanation. "Just you wait until I get you!..." he yelled.

He rushed at the pair waving his arms fiercely. The mischievous man and his mischievous wife ran as fast as they could into the shelter of the forest, with all the villagers rushing after them.

When they reached the forest, the mischievous man and his mischievous wife climbed up a tree to hide from the villagers. For a few minutes the villagers chasing them were puzzled. Then one of them spotted the mischievous wife's hair hanging down from a branch.

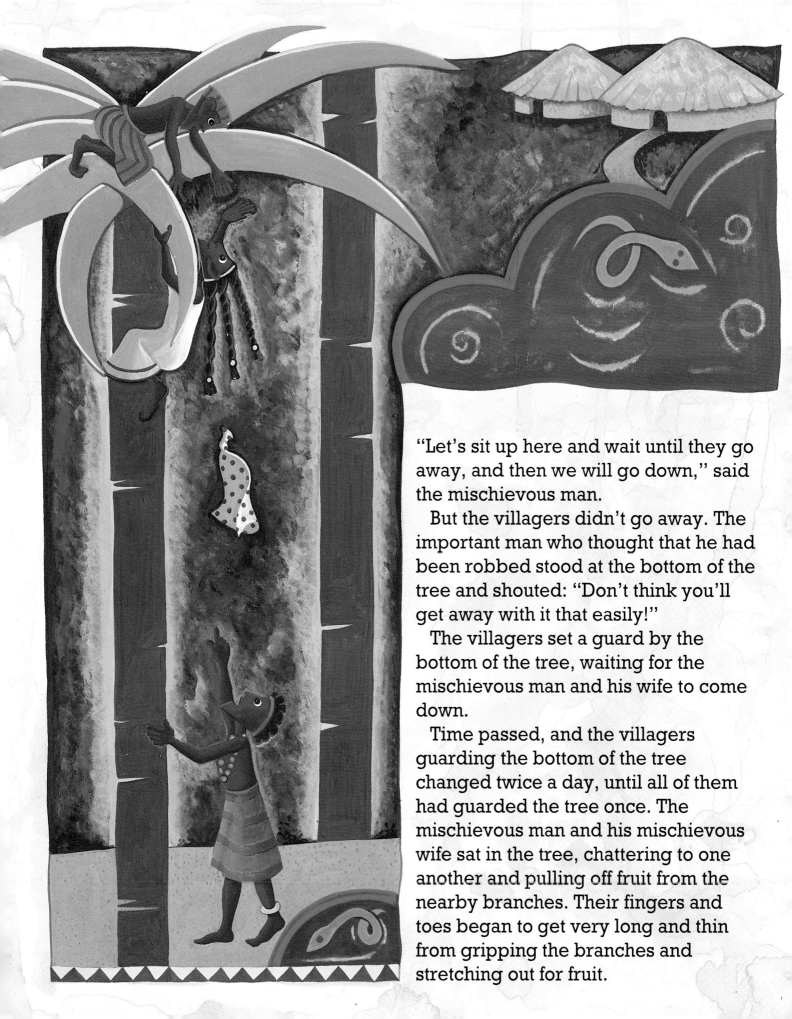

"Let's sit up here and wait until they go away, and then we will go down," said the mischievous man.

But the villagers didn't go away. The important man who thought that he had been robbed stood at the bottom of the tree and shouted: "Don't think you'll get away with it that easily!"

The villagers set a guard by the bottom of the tree, waiting for the mischievous man and his wife to come down.

Time passed, and the villagers guarding the bottom of the tree changed twice a day, until all of them had guarded the tree once. The mischievous man and his mischievous wife sat in the tree, chattering to one another and pulling off fruit from the nearby branches. Their fingers and toes began to get very long and thin from gripping the branches and stretching out for fruit.

One day, when all the villagers had guarded the bottom of the tree twice, the mischievous man and his mischievous wife realized that the hair on their bodies had grown long and thick, making it hard for them to be seen in the branches.

One day, when all the villagers had guarded the bottom of the tree three times, the mischievous man and his mischievous wife felt a funny sensation at the bottom of their spines. They had grown tails! They jumped up and down on their branch, chattering to one another very fast and swinging with their new tails.

The villager at the bottom of the tree heard all the noise and stared up at the pair. What a surprise he got! The mischievous man and his mischievous wife had turned into monkeys!

When the villager went back to the village to tell the others what he had seen, the important man who thought he had been robbed was furious. But later, when he had counted his cowrie shells, he realized how unjust he had been. How he regretted his hastiness!

And that is why, even though the people of the Congo are often annoyed with mischievous monkeys who come into their houses and make a mess or take their food, they never harm them.

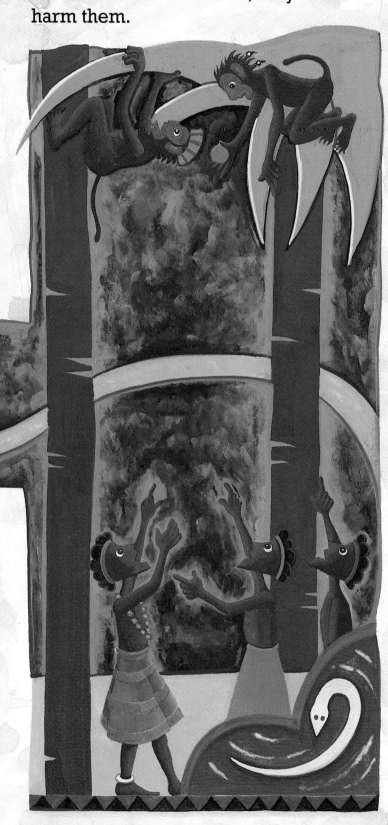

TRUE OR FALSE?

Which of these facts are true and which ones are false? If you have read this book carefully, you will know the answers.

1. Rain forests are found all over Europe.

2. Rain forests lie between the tropics of Capricorn and Cancer.

3. There are up to 40 kinds of rain forests.

4. Orangutans are found in the forests of Africa.

5. As many as 280 tree species have been counted in one $2^1/_2$-acre (1-hectare) area of rain forest.

6. The world's largest rain forest is in Australia.

7. Algae and insects shelter in the long fur of the sloth.

8. Giant eagles feed on animals from the forest floor.

9. Chickens originally came from the rain forest.

10. Tribespeople collect poison from rain forest frogs by squeezing them.

11. Sap from a tree in the Amazon basin can be used as diesel fuel in trucks.

12. Slash-and-burn farming helps the soil to grow richer.

13. The rain forests may be destroyed by the year 2050.

Answers: 1. False 2. True 3. True 4. False 5. True 6. False 7. True 8. False 9. True 10. False 11. True 12. False 13. True

Polar Lands

LOOKING AT THE POLES

Few areas in the world are as harsh and desolate as the North and South poles, and few are as beautiful. For much of the year both areas are freezing cold, with fierce winds and thick snow and ice on the ground. As it grows colder even the seas freeze.

Not many animals live here. Some species, however, are hardy enough to live, breed, and find food in the open wastes. Their bodies have specially adapted to the constant cold.

In the summer months, May to July at the North Pole and November to January at the South Pole, the sun shines even at midnight. In winter, the poles remain almost permanently dark.

The snow and ice recede in the short summers, leaving the ground littered with pools of **meltwater**. The land is covered with flowers and bursts of green leaves. Creatures mate and nest or find safe places to give birth to their young. The air is filled with insects.

▶ Plants in the polar lands spend most of the time under snow but burst into life during the short summer. Their seeds are very hardy and do not **germinate** until the conditions around them are exactly right for growth.

▼ A large **iceberg** floats in the summer sea off Antarctica. It is sunset, but at this time of year the sky never really grows dark.

WHERE IN THE WORLD?

The poles are at the top and bottom of the earth. Because they are farther from the sun than any other point on earth, the sun's rays are weaker, which makes the polar lands colder than anywhere else in the world.

At the North Pole lies a frozen sea, called the Arctic Ocean. This ocean is surrounded by Europe, Asia, and North America. The most northerly point where trees will grow is about 1,429 miles (2,300 kilometers) from the North Pole. Between the **tree line** and the **icecap** lie regions of **tundra**, which is rough terrain covered with rugged vegetation. The layer of earth beneath the tundra is always frozen, even in summer. It is called **permafrost**.

The continent of Antarctica lies at the South Pole and is permanently covered in **ice sheets** known as the Antarctic icecap.

HISTORY OF THE POLES

150-170 million years ago
The poles are not frozen. The South Pole may lie over low ground and the North Pole over open ocean.

60-70 million years ago
Shifts in the earth's plates cause the poles to move to the positions where they now lie. They begin to cool.

5-6 million years ago
The polar lands are still quite warm at sea level. Changes in the climate and in the heat received from the sun bring new conditions of snow and ice, which have been there ever since.

NORTH POLE FACTS

● Because the North Pole is surrounded by land, warmer currents from close to the equator never reach the Arctic Ocean to warm it.

● The ancient Greeks named the Arctic after the constellation of the Great Bear, which they called Arktos.

● Americans Robert Peary and Matthew Henson were the first explorers to reach the North Pole in 1909.

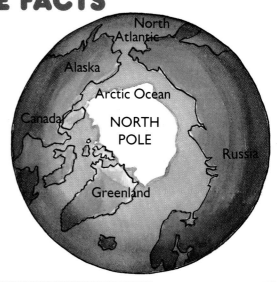

Snow and ice lie deeper here than anywhere else in the world.

The poles were not always such cold places. Fossils of trees, plants, and dinosaurs found in Antarctica show that it once had a much warmer climate. Movements of the **plates** that make up the earth's surface, together with the

▲ A herd of caribou passes along the northern treeline on its annual journey to richer feeding grounds.

warming and cooling of our planet over many centuries, have finally brought about the chilly conditions we know at the poles today.

SOUTH POLE FACTS

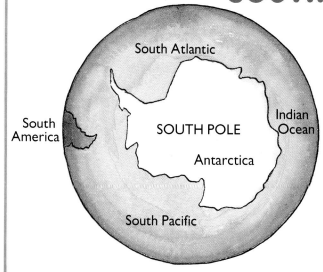

South Atlantic

South America

SOUTH POLE

Indian Ocean

Antarctica

South Pacific

● Seventy-five percent of the world's water is stored in glaciers, and most of this lies in the Antarctic icecap.

● The Antarctic can be called a desert, as it receives less than 6 inches (150 millimeters) of rain or snow per year.

● Norwegian Roald Amundsen beat Britain's Robert Scott to the South Pole by five weeks in 1911.

FROZEN FEATURES

One-fourth of the world's oceans and seas are affected by ice every year. Most of this comes in the form of icebergs. An Antarctic iceberg has reached almost as far as Rio de Janeiro, a journey of 3,440 miles (5,500 kilometers).

At the South Pole, ice covers the land and forms cliffs and **glaciers**. As the ice in the glaciers becomes old and heavy, it moves slowly forward and reaches the sea after many years. Long tongues of this glacier extend out into the sea, and large chunks of ice break off. This ice floats away to become new icebergs.

◀ Paradise Bay Glacier in the Antarctic. Sections break off from these craggy cliffs and plummet into the clear waters below to form new icebergs.

Icebergs are made from frozen fresh water, but at the poles the salty ocean freezes, too. This reaches a peak in February and March, when there is about 4.5 million square miles (12 million square kilometers) of sea ice in the Arctic Ocean and 1 million square miles (3 million square kilometers) off Antarctica.

As the sea freezes, a greasy film appears to cover the water. A curtain of wispy "smoke" rises from the surface and, as the seawater turns to ice, salt is pushed above the surface in beautiful crystals called **ice flowers**.

Ever since the sinking of the ocean liner the Titanic by an iceberg in 1912, in which 1,517 lives were lost, the International Ice Patrol has kept watch on icebergs to alert ships to possible danger in the ocean.

DIFFERENT KINDS OF ICE

● As the sea freezes, the first ice to form is not very solid. It is called **frazil ice**. As the salt content is pushed out, thick **pancake ice** forms. Finally slabs of ice freeze together to form **pack ice**.

● Glacier bergs have broken off glaciers that run into the sea. This is dense, ancient ice. As it is so heavy, only about one-tenth shows above the water's surface.

● **Tabular icebergs** have broken off from ice shelves. They have flat tops and are sometimes used by scientists as convenient research bases.

● Fragments of ice are called **brash ice**. Large fragments from the **icecap** are called **bergy bits**, and smaller pieces are known as **growlers**.

ANIMAL LIFE

Despite the bleakness of the polar lands, many animals live there, either all year around or as summer visitors when the temperature rises to 50°F (10°C) above freezing.

On the Antarctic icecap most of the permanent residents are insects. On the very edge of the ice there are penguins, seals, and migratory birds, while the sea is filled with an abundance of life.

An enormous variety of animals live in the Arctic, from the tiny shrew to the huge polar bear. Native species are well adapted to make use of the short summer and protect themselves against the long winter. Polar animals tend to be larger than their cousins in warmer climates. They have short legs, long hair, and an undercoat of dense

▲ The stoat, like many other animals grows a white **pelt** during the winter. This helps to **camouflage** it against the snow when it hunts.

▼ Polar bear cubs are born in pairs and stay with their mother for up to 2 years. Polar bears may live up to 33 years in the wild.

▶ Seals come in many shapes and sizes. They are superbly adapted to life in and out of water. Seals are torpedo-shaped to help them glide easily through the water. Their bodies are covered in a thick layer of **blubber**, which protects their internal organs from the cold. This blubber is between 1 and 6 inches (2.5 and 15 centimeters) thick and gives seals energy when there is no food available.

fur. Their tails are short, and the pads on their large feet are furry.

Every 10 to 13 years small mammals such as lemmings or voles breed in enormous numbers. With such a ready supply of food available, larger meat-eaters also grow in number. Eventually there is little vegetation for the small mammals to eat, and many of them die. The larger animals then also suffer a large population drop, and the vegetation begins to grow back.

◀ A pack of wolves follows its leader into the treeline. A wolf can see and smell its prey more than 1 mile (1.6 kilometers) away. Most wolves have gray fur, but the Arctic wolf may grow pure white fur for camouflage against the snow.

Wolves can eat up to 20 pounds (9 kilograms) of food at one time. However, they can go without eating for two weeks or longer.

BIRDLAND

The polar winter is too cold for most birds. But during the summer many species of birds arrive. The Arctic tern flies from summer at one pole to summer at the other. It covers a distance of 18,750 miles (30,000 kilometers) every year. Other birds include geese, ducks, and smaller birds such as larks and pipits. On the surface lie pools of melted ice and snow where millions of mosquitoes and other insects flourish. The humming air is a feast for birds!

During the winter, a number of birds live on the **subarctic** wastes of the tundra, where they live by searching for roots and berries under the snow or by feeding on other birds, small mammals, or insects. Here in the north live the ptarmigan, the snowy owl, and, close to the tree line, the raven and Arctic redpoll.

Throughout the Antarctic year, birds such as penguins remain hardy in all conditions. A penguin can dive as deep as 164 feet (50 meters) underwater in search of fish. This is the height of a 24-story building! King penguins must return to land every five to six weeks during the winter to feed their growing young. The adults then cluster together on the shore. The cold penguins from the edge of the group exchange places with the warmed birds from the center every few minutes. Their young soon grow into enormous brown furry lumps of some 26 pounds (12 kilograms) in body weight but have to fast for up to a month at a time while their parents are out at sea. By the spring they weigh no more than 13 pounds (6 kilograms). Many chicks die during this period.

◄ The largest of the penguin family is the Emperor. It stands more than 3 feet (1 meter) tall and weighs up to 90 pounds (40 kilograms). The male penguin **incubates** the eggs in a special pouch on his feet. He will go as long as two months without eating.

▲ A black-browed albatross flies over the Antarctic Ocean. It has long, thin wings, which help it to glide through the air.

▼ Puffins fly to the Arctic during the summer and nest among the rocky cliffs surrounding the frozen ocean.

SEA LIFE

Below the waves and ice of the polar oceans, the temperature remains far more constant than at the surface. For this reason, creatures such as polar bears, seals, and penguins prefer to spend as much time as possible diving and swimming.

In the Antarctic the stable temperature and warm currents from more temperate zones encourage many varieties of colorful growth. Bright orange sea spiders, delicate anemones, fronds of primitive weeds, worms, and other strange creatures litter the sea floor.

Strange ghostly fish live here, too, like the pale ice-fish or transparent deep-sea angler. In areas under the ice where little light filters through to

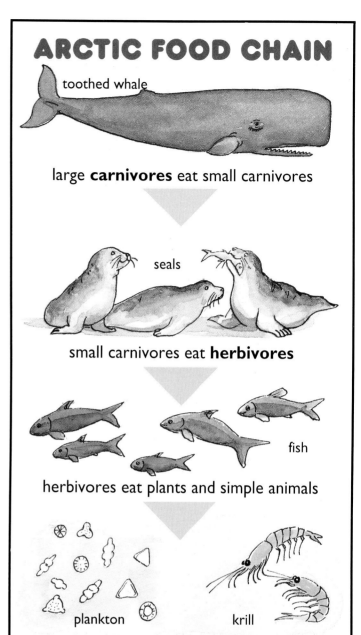

ARCTIC FOOD CHAIN

toothed whale

large **carnivores** eat small carnivores

seals

small carnivores eat **herbivores**

fish

herbivores eat plants and simple animals

plankton   krill

This is a food chain of polar animals living in the sea. Smaller animals tend to be eaten by larger animals. Herbivores eat only plants or simple life such as krill. At the bottom of the chain, plants and simple animals do not need to eat major organisms to stay alive.

◀ Krill are tiny crustaceans similar to shrimp. Some countries, including Japan, have recently begun fishing for krill to provide food for people. This mass harvesting of krill poses a threat to the creatures of polar lands, which rely on them as a primary food source.

the depths, these creatures have no need of bright coloring. Many carry an internal light source, supplied by bacteria carried in a special gland.

The largest marine animals, the whales, live mainly in the Antarctic. Biggest of all are the blue whales, which grow up to 98 feet (30 meters) long and weigh 14.8 tons (150,000 kilograms). They are the largest animals on earth. There are two groups of whales: **toothed whales**, which feed on fish and seals, and **baleen whales**, which feed on tiny creatures called krill. Baleen whales have a series of bony plates in their mouths, which helps them sift the krill from the water.

▶ This killer whale is breaching. Killer whales are members of the dolphin family. They can swim as fast as 25 miles per hour (40 kilometers per hour). They swim in all oceans but prefer polar waters.

◀ This giant sea spider has 10 legs. It lives on the ocean floor near the South Pole. Sea spiders have between 4 and 10 legs. They are not members of the same family group as land spiders, all of which have 8 legs.

The bodies of sea spiders are so small that some of the spiders' food is digested in their legs!

PEOPLE OF THE POLES

On the icecap of Antarctica there are no human residents. Only scientists brave these regions to carry out their experiments.

In the Arctic, however, local peoples have learned how to survive in the harsh climate. Many still live as **nomads**, following the herds of animals that provide their livelihood, although today many of them have a fixed home in one of the settlements.

The Inuit, or Eskimo as they are sometimes known, live in North America and Russia and are the largest group. Few still drive sleds

▼ Igloos are now mostly built as overnight resting places on long hunting trips. They are built from large slabs of ice, carefully cut to size and placed together for a snug fit against the winds. Traditional lighting came from whale or seal oil burned in a small container. This also efficiently heated the room.

pulled by husky dogs or wear the traditional stitched animal skins. Most prefer to ride over the icecap on engine-driven snowmobiles and to wear anoraks; although the stitched skins are, in fact, even warmer.

Today the closely related Inuit tribes of Alaska and Russia are allowed to meet without regard to political boundaries. Changes in the way Eastern Europe is governed mean that people living there are able to visit other countries more freely than under the old laws.

The people of the North may in the future find it easier to fish and hunt where the animals wander and not where governments force them to live.

PEOPLE FACTS

● The Yahgans and Onas, who used to live in the Antarctic region at the tip of South America, have died out.

● Arctic people eat mostly fish and meat, as there is little plant life available.

● More than 100,000 Inuit are spread over four countries along the Arctic coastline.

▲ An Inuit man wearing his traditional costume of boots, leggings, trousers, hooded jacket, and mitts. These are made from the skins of animals such as caribou, bear, or wolf. The clothes are made loose-fitting to allow an extra layer of warm air around the body. The seams are tightly sewn to waterproof the garment.

WATCHING THE WEATHER

Polar lands are useful places to study the weather, because the temperature at the poles affects climates all over the world. It is the cold air blowing from the poles and meeting the hot air from the equator that causes our weather patterns. Scientists can also find out about patterns in the world's climate that existed thousands of

▼ This map shows major cities around the world that will be in serious danger of being submerged by the sea if the polar icecaps melt as a result of global warming. Even world centers such as London or New York would be lost beneath the waters.

THE EARTH'S ATMOSPHERE

mesosphere

stratosphere

troposphere

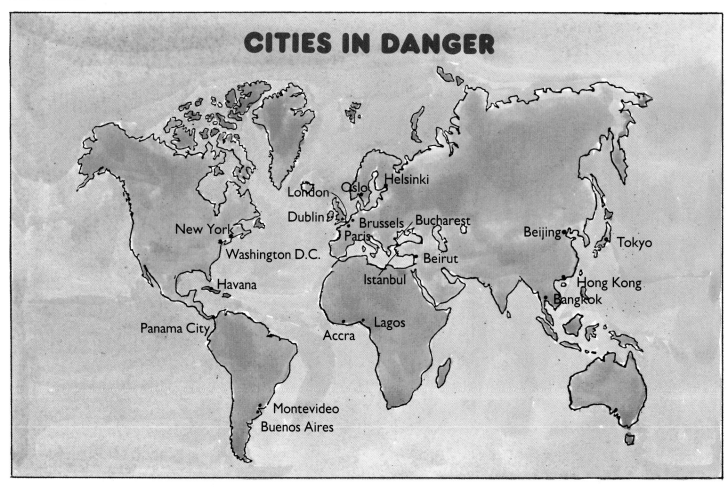

CITIES IN DANGER

Helsinki
London
Oslo
Dublin
New York
Brussels
Bucharest
Paris
Beijing
Tokyo
Washington D.C.
Beirut
Havana
Istanbul
Hong Kong
Bangkok
Panama City
Lagos
Accra
Montevideo
Buenos Aires

years ago by studying the ice that has lain at the poles since that time.

The world is warming up for many reasons. Chief among these is the growing hole in the **ozone layer** at each pole, where it is thickest. This is the layer within the stratosphere layer of the earth's atmosphere that protects us from the sun's harmful ultraviolet rays. The ozone is being destroyed by human-made chemicals including chlorofluorocarbons (CFCs), which are used in aerosol sprays.

Global warming is also increased by the effect of **greenhouse gases**. Gases produced by industrial processes are building up in the earth's atmosphere. These gases act as a blanket, trapping

▲ The aurora borealis is a beautiful and rare sight seen mainly near the North Pole. It is caused by the entry of solar particles into the earth's magnetic field. A similar phenomenon in the Antarctic is known as the aurora australis.

HOW YOU CAN HELP THE WORLD

● Give up using aerosol sprays which contain CFCs. Look out for alternatives that are now widespread in supermarkets. Most are pumps and are labeled "ozone friendly" or "CFC free."

● Ask adults to compost garden waste instead of burning it. Chemicals in the smoke pollute the atmosphere. And compost helps new plants to grow.

● Try to persuade adults to run their cars on leadfree gasoline. A car that runs on gasoline containing lead releases into the atmosphere its own weight in carbon dioxide fumes every year.

heat from the sun instead of allowing it to be reflected back into space.

As the world grows warmer, so the oceans around the poles grow more hospitable. At present, polar temperatures rise only to 50°F (10°C) at the very height of summer. If the temperature were to rise by more than five percent at the poles, the ice would melt and sea levels across the world could rise drastically. Low-lying cities such as London and New York as well as whole countries such as the Netherlands and Bangladesh could be flooded. At these temperatures many of the specialized animals and plants of the polar regions would die out, too.

EXPLOITING THE POLES

The first outsiders to see potential for making money in the poles came during the 1800's. They killed whales in great numbers for their meat and for their blubber, which was used in a variety of products from soap to oil. Seals, particularly fur seals, were trapped for their attractive pelts. Penguins were killed, because their oil was useful as a light source.

Today international agreements are in force to protect the creatures of the poles from hunters. A few animals are still killed each year for scientific purposes, and local peoples are also permitted to hunt and kill a number of animals.

Animals face other dangers, too. Polar bears are great scavengers and may become too dependent on scientific bases for scraps of food. They can often be seen in garbage dumps, where they sometimes eat unsuitable things, cut themselves on sharp edges, or lose the will to hunt.

Extra industrial activity at the poles may also add to the world's environmental problems. The glaring white surface of the icecap at each pole helps to reflect back into space hot rays from the sun.

Pale colors bounce rays off their surface. Bright, shiny snow is very good at doing this. Dark colors soak in warm rays of light and grow hotter. This is why you may prefer to wear light-colored clothes to help you stay cool in the hot summer.

POLAR RESOURCES

● Ninety-eight percent of Antarctica is covered by thick ice, but beneath may lie valuable deposits of rubies and other minerals.

● Reserves of oil and natural gas lie under Alaska, Arctic Canada, and Siberia. Further oil deposits are found off the coast of Greenland, on the Arctic shores of the North Atlantic, and in parts of the Antarctic Ocean.

● Oil spillage from a tanker accident in Alaska in the spring of 1989 killed many birds and other animals.

◀ The bleached-white bones of long-dead whales remind us of the years when these great mammals were hunted mercilessly. The bowhead whale was even called the "right" whale because it was so easy to catch.

▲ A polar bear forages among the discarded litter of a modern settlement in northern Canada. He could be poisoned or injured and also poses a serious threat to the local people.

Some scientists fear that dust and grime from industrial processes might make the ice darker, thereby reflecting fewer rays than at present. This would trap heat in the earth's atmosphere and increase the effects of global warming.

If people attempt to melt the permafrost to mine minerals and other resources, there may also be the danger that modern structures such as buildings, railroads, or vital oil-relaying pipelines will be ruined.

SAVING THE POLES

It is important that human beings realize the importance of keeping the polar lands clean for the future. The specialized animals and plants will die if the temperatures are allowed to rise.

Sensible measures have been taken to establish both the North and South poles as areas of special scientific interest rather than purely as areas to be exploited. The first legal restraint on animal slaughter in these regions was passed by Great Britain in 1904. Since then many other nations have joined to save threatened species.

The long-standing Antarctic Treaty concerning ownership of the lands of the South Pole was agreed upon by most of the world's governments.

Even industry has taken steps to avoid future damage to this most desolate of the world parks. Special ice roads have been built to protect slow-growing plants from being crushed under the wheels of a succession of heavy vehicles.

Similarly, oil and gas pipelines are built up off the ground like bridges. Despite people's continuing encroachment on the lands of the poles, the caribou in the North may continue their migration in peace.

▲ A rookery of King penguins shows the efficiency of creatures that have adapted to extreme conditions. If the poles become warmer, the penguins may not survive.

▶ An aerial view of the snow-crusted ridges of Greenland. The world would lose one of its great natural beauties if we allow the destruction of the polar icecaps.

CROW STEALS SOME DAYLIGHT

For thousands of years people have told stories about the world around them. Often these stories try to explain something that people do not really understand, like how the world began or where light comes from. This tale is told by the Inuit who live in the polar lands of northern Canada.

Long ago, in the northern lands where the Inuit live, there was no daylight. The people ate, slept, went hunting, and cooked all in darkness. There was no light to tell the people which was day and which was night, so they all got up at different times. When they needed to see they

day he told them about a land where light shone all day and people could see without using a lamp and could spot animals far off. The villagers were amazed at this and began to realize how difficult their lives were without light during the day.

would light little seal-oil lamps, which gave off a small glimmer of light, scarcely enough to see by.

In one village lived a wise old Crow. He used to tell the people stories of the far-off lands that he had visited. One

"When we go fishing," said one, "we have to shine a light into the holes we make in the ice to see if any fish are there, and that scares the fish off. If it were light all the time, we would be able to see the fish before they saw us."

"And without light," said another, "we are quite likely to walk straight into the arms of a polar bear before we even realize that it's there. If it were light all the time, we would be able to see polar bears in the distance and keep away."

All the villagers begged the Crow to go to the land of daylight and fetch them some light. At first the Crow said no, because it was such a long journey. But the villagers had always been very good to him, so eventually he agreed.

It was a very long journey indeed and when, at last, the Crow reached the eastern lands where the sky was bright with daylight, he sank to the ground, exhausted. He found himself in a village not so very different from the one he had left. In the middle of the village was a house from which daylight shone brightly.

"Aha!" thought the Crow. "That is where the daylight comes from."

As he watched, a woman walked up to the house. The Crow flew over to the door, shook off his skin, and turned himself into a speck of dust, which settled on the woman's dress as she went into the house.

Inside the house a great chief sat watching a baby playing on a fur rug. As the woman passed she bent down and tickled the baby. She didn't notice the tiny speck of dust fall from her dress and into the little baby's ear. It was the Crow of course!

The baby tugged at his ear, which tickled dreadfully, and began to cry, whereupon the chief and the woman

leapt up and began to fuss over him.

"Ask for some daylight," whispered the speck of dust.

So the baby cried for some daylight. The chief picked up a carved wooden box, placed it before the baby, and opened the lid. Inside were seven glowing balls of daylight. The chief took out one of the balls and gave it to the baby. The baby was so delighted with the new toy that all his tears were gone at once.

"Ask for a string to be tied to the ball," whispered the speck of dust in the baby's ear.

And the baby began to cry for a string to be tied to the beautiful ball of daylight.

No sooner had the chief tied a string to the ball and given it to the baby, than the little speck of dust whispered in the baby's ear again.

"Move over to the doorway."

The baby crawled over to the hut's doorway, trailing the ball of daylight on the string, and sat, framed by the arch, with daylight shining brightly all around.

Gradually the baby moved farther and farther out of the house, dangling the ball, right to the very spot where the Crow had left his skin, Quick as a flash, the speck of dust fell out of the baby's ear, picked up the skin, and became the Crow again. The Crow snatched the string from the baby and flew off, carrying away the bright ball of daylight.

The baby began to scream and cry,

and all the villagers came rushing out of their houses. They threw stones at the Crow and tried to shoot him down with their bows and arrows, but the Crow flew off toward the west much too fast for them.

When, at last, the Crow came to the land of the Inuit, he broke off a piece of daylight from the ball over each village that he passed and let it fall. Finally, after much traveling, he reached the village that he had set off from. Then he let go of the string, and all that was left of the ball of daylight fell to the ground and shattered. Shafts of light streamed

into all the houses. The villagers rushed out of their houses to thank the Crow for his wonderful gift.

The Crow told the story of how he had stolen the light. And he explained to all the villagers that he had not brought enough light for them to have daylight all the time, but only enough for daylight half the year and that the other half of the year they would have darkness.

"But if I had brought enough daylight for it to be always light," he said, "you would have had as much trouble as you did when it was always dark!"

TRUE OR FALSE?

Which of these facts are true and which ones are false? If you have read this book carefully, you will know the answers.

1. Summer falls between May and July at both poles.

2. No plants grow in the polar lands.

3. Plants and animals once lived in a warmer climate on Antarctica.

4. The Arctic was named by the Ancient Greeks after the constellation of the Plough.

5. The Norwegian Roald Amundsen was the first person to reach the South Pole.

6. *The Titanic* sank in 1912 after running into a blue whale.

7. Large fragments from the ice sheet are called bergy growlers.

8. The largest permanent residents on the Antarctic ice sheet are insects.

9. A male Emperor penguin will go as long as four months without food.

10. Polar bear cubs are born two at a time.

11. Arctic people are mostly vegetarian.

12. A car running on gasoline containing lead releases its own weight in carbon dioxide fumes every year.

GLOSSARY

Acid rain is rain polluted by chemicals released from industrial waste, car exhaust, and burning fuel. It can poison trees and plants and erode the face of buildings.

Altitude is the measurement of height above sea level.

Arid land is parched soil with sparse vegetation. Little rain falls on this type of land and it is prone to desertification.

An **avalanche** is caused when heavy snow slips down a mountainside. It can damage property and injure people and animals.

Baleen whales have a curtain of bony plates in their mouths. These allow them to sift the tiny krill on which they feed from the ocean.

Bay is a part of an ocean or other large body of water that forms a curve in the shoreline. It is bordered on the coastline by headlands or capes.

Bergy bits are large sections that have broken off the icecap.

Blubber is the name for the thick layer of fat on animals such as seals, walruses, penguins, and whales. This layer helps to protect them against the cold. In the past it was used to make goods such as soap and oil for household lighting.

Brash ice is the name for small fragments of ice.

Bushmen are people who live in desert lands, such as in

Africa or Australia. They drink little, as they obtain enough moisture from eating underground roots and desert melons.

Buttress roots develop to support heavy tree trunks and help keep the tall trees of the rain forest upright.

Camouflage is the method by which the body surface of certain creatures is covered in patterns or colors that matches its background. These help to hide the animals from predators. A chameleon can change its body color so that it is always the same as the background it walks against. The coat of an Arctic fox is white and makes the fox invisible from a distance against the snow.

Canopy is the uppermost layer of the rain forest. It is the dense leafy section some 18 to 21 feet (6 to 7 meters) deep and 120 to 150 feet (40 to 50 meters) above ground.

Carnivores are meat-eating animals.

Coniferous trees produce cones and are evergreen. They are found mainly in the Northern Hemisphere. A coniferous forest is made up of only evergreen trees.

Conservation is the special protection and preservation of wildlife and environments that have been exploited by humans. It involves help from governments and scientists.

A **continent** is a piece of land, or mainland. It is larger than a normal island and is divided into several countries, except for the continent of Australia. Two or more continents may be joined together by a narrow neck of land.

A **coral reef** is a colorful ridge formation, usually underwater. It is made up of the hard outer casing produced by a colony of millions of tiny animals known as polyps.

The **core** is the center of the earth. It is thought to be solid and is likely to be made of iron and nickel.

Courtship display is when a bird, an animal, or an insect performs or changes color to attract a mate.

The **crust** is the earth's thin surface layer. Mountains are built in the crust.

A **current** or stream is the movement of a body of water in a particular direction. Ocean currents may be strong and extend over great distances.

Deciduous trees lose all of their leaves before a cold or dry season. They cannot live in very cold climates, unlike coniferous trees. A deciduous forest is made up of only deciduous trees.

Deforestation is the destruction of large areas of woodland to make room for building, mining, or farming.

A **desert** is a place with little vegetation where less than 10 inches (25 centimeters) of rain falls each year.

Desertification is the process by which dry areas of land on the edge of deserts suffer from drought and also become desert. If regular rainfall returns to the area, the new region of desert could recover.

Domesticated animals are those which have been bred by humans over many generations to be tame and, in some cases, to provide products such as meat, milk, leather, and wool.

Drip-tip is the long tip on most leaves in the rain forest that sheds rain from the leaf's waxy surface.

A **drought** is a period when little or no rain falls. Crops do not grow, water is scarce, and animals and humans find it hard to survive.

An **echo** is the repetition of a noise caused by the bouncing back of sound waves from a solid object. Marine mammals use echoes to locate food and to avoid obstacles.

An **ecosystem** is a community of plants and animals and their environment.

Environment is the particular combination of conditions in an area, which affects the type of living things inhabiting it. An animal's survival depends on how well it can respond in these conditions.

Ephemerals are tiny plants that survive as seeds in dry conditions such as desert sands. During a period of heavy rain they burst into flower.

Epiphyte is a plant that grows on another plant without damaging it.

Equator is the imaginary line around the earth, exactly halfway between the North and South poles.

Erosion is the wearing away, or eroding, of soil or land by wind or water. Trees help to prevent erosion.

Evaporation is when water turns into tiny droplets of vapor in the air. This process happens each morning to the dew that has fallen during the night in the hot desert.

Evergreen trees and plants drop and then replace their leaves throughout the year. This means that they always look green. They can grow in colder climates than deciduous trees.

Extinct means that the last member of an animal or plant species has died out as a result of overhunting, a change in its habitat, or its failure to compete with a new animal or plant.

Famine is a period when food is scarce and many people and animals starve and die. This often takes place after a drought, when crops have been unable to grow.

Fault-block mountains are formed when a block of rock

is forced up a crack, or fault, in the earth's crust. It often has a flat surface on top called a plateau, which is similar to a plain.

Fertile land is land which is good for growing lush and healthy crops.

Fold mountains are formed when rock is crumpled and forced upward as the edges of two or more of the earth's plates meet and grind together.

Frazil ice is the first thin ice that forms as the sea begins to freeze.

Germination is the moment when plant seeds come out of their dormant state as a result of suitable conditions for growth and begin to sprout.

Glacier is a river of ice that moves very slowly. It is

pushed by new ice that forms on high ground.

Greenhouse gases, such as carbon dioxide, collect in the earth's atmosphere. They trap the heat rays from the sun and prevent them from bouncing back into outer space. As a result of the greenhouse effect, the earth's climate is growing warmer.

Growlers are small pieces that have broken away from an icecap.

A **gulf** is a part of a sea or ocean that loops into the neighboring coastline. It has a narrower mouth than a bay.

A **habitat** is the natural environment of a plant or animal.

Hardwood trees, such as ebony, teak, and mahogany, grow in the rain forest. Their tough wood is excellent for making strong furniture, and this is one cause of the destruction of large parts of the rain forest.

Herbivores are plant-eating animals.

Hibernate is what some animals do in cold weather to survive. They fatten themselves during the warmer months, then sleep all through the long winter. While hibernating, animals use little energy, and many do not need food.

Hunter-gatherers are people who live off the land by harvesting food from the plants and animals that live there. They are skillful in taking only what the land can survive without.

Ice flowers form when salt is pushed out as the sea freezes. The salt forms strange arrangements of beautiful crystals.

Ice sheet is another name for the Arctic and Antarctic shields of ice.

Iceberg is a large lump of ice that floats in the sea. Many icebergs break off from glaciers that slowly pour into the sea. Only one-tenth of these icebergs usually show above the surface of the water.

Icecap is the name for the huge shield of ice that covers both the Arctic Ocean and Antarctica.

Incubation is the time between the laying of a bird's egg and its hatching.

Irrigation is the method by which farmers water land that naturally tends to be dry. Water is often channeled over land through ditches

or retained on land with a hard, resistant surface such as low walls.

Land-locked areas of water are surrounded by land.

Larvae are the young of some insect species before they develop and grow wings.

Latitude is a line drawn from east to west on a map.

The **mantle** is the layer of rock surrounding the earth's core, lying beneath the crust.

Marine means related to the sea. Marine animals are those that live in the sea.

Meltwater is the water that appears when ice and snow melt during the polar summer. Meltwater may cause flooding.

To **migrate** is to travel long distances every year. Many

birds migrate from summer breeding grounds to warmer winter feeding places.

A **mineral** is a chemical compound found in rocks. Some minerals are useful to humans and are mined.

Mixed woodlands are forests with evergreen conifers as well as seasonal deciduous trees.

A **native** is a plant, animal, or person whose family originally comes from the area in which it lives.

Nomads are people who travel from one area to another, either to take their herds of animals to fresh grazing or to escape severe weather, such as cold or drought. They feed mainly on products from their herds and often live in tents, which can easily be packed up and

carried on the next journey. The Lapps of northern Scandinavia travel in this way, tending their reindeer.

Ozone layer prevents the sun's harmful ultraviolet rays from entering the earth's atmosphere. A hole in this layer is forming over each pole, where it is thickest.

Pack ice is formed when slabs of thick sea ice freeze together.

Pancake ice is created when the salt is pushed out of freezing seawater. It often forms in round shapes with raised edges, like pancakes.

A **pearl** is a small gem, usually round and white, cream, or bluish-gray. It slowly forms as a protective layer around a grain of sand or other object that irritates the soft flesh inside an oyster's shell.

Pelt is the name for an animal's fur.

Permafrost is an underground layer of soil that remains frozen all year, even during the polar summer.

Pesticides are chemicals used to kill pests that feed on crops. Pesticides may sometimes be dangerous to creatures other than the pests they control.

Plankton is the rich 'soup' found in areas of water which is made up of many types of microscopic life. A large variety of sea animals feeds on plankton.

A **plateau** is the flat area at the top of a fault-block mountain.

Plates are huge sections of rock in the earth's crust on which the continents float.

These plates move slowly over hundreds and thousands of years. The continents move with them. As the plates meet and their edges grind against each other, volcanoes erupt and earthquakes occur.

The **poles** are found at the exact north and south ends of the earth. Day and night each last six months at the poles.

A **pollutant** is a dirty and poisonous product, such as car fumes, that damages the environment.

To **pollute** means to poison air, land or water. Pollution is often caused by the waste from human industrial activity.

Predators are animals that hunt and kill other creatures for food.

Rain forests are thick, evergreen forests with high levels of rainfall. Temperate rain forests are warm and moist with most rainfall in winter. Tropical rain forests are hot and wet with heavy rainfall all year around.

Rain shadow is the area on a mountainside facing away from the sea. It receives little rain. Most of the rain falls over the seaward side of the mountain.

Reproduction is when adult creatures produce new, young individuals for the continuation of their species.

Resources are the natural materials taken from their environment and used by people, for example, wood.

Rodents are small mammals, such as squirrels and beavers, with strong front teeth which they use for gnawing hard objects.

Scavenge is to feed on the refuse left by others, for instance, to feed on another animal's kill.

Scrubland is territory where vegetation grows low and stunted.

Slash-and-burn farming is practiced by poor farmers who clear areas of the rain forest for soil on which to grow their crops. These farmers move on every few seasons, as the soil holds little good once the trees have gone.

Snowline is the level on the side of a mountain above which no plant life can grow. Snow often covers the mountain above this level all the year round.

Species is a group of animals or plants that shares the same characteristics and can breed with one another.

Subarctic describes the area south of the Arctic, which is almost as cold in winter but much warmer in summer.

Tabular icebergs have a large, flat surface, like that of a table.

Taproots are long, thin roots that push their way through the layers of stone beneath the sand. They help some desert trees find moisture during long periods of drought.

Territory is the area where an animal lives and breeds.

Tides are the regular rise and fall of the sea, caused by the pull of the moon and the sun.

Toothed whales have peglike teeth on their lower jaws. They eat animals such as seals, squid, and fish.

Topsoil is the uppermost and richest layer of earth where most plants grow. The desert lacks topsoil, which has dried out due to lack of rain and has been blown away by the wind. In the rain forest, the topsoil lies above the stony ground beneath the rain forest floor. This rich earth is held in place by the rain forest trees, but is rapidly washed away by rain when the trees are cut down.

Toxic means poisonous and harmful to life.

Treeline is the level on a mountainside above which the climate is too cold and windy for trees to grow. It is the farthest point to the north on a map.

A **trench** is a deep furrow. The Mariana Trench near Guam is the deepest known place in any ocean.

Tribe is a community of people who live together for protection from danger and for a shared way of life.

Tropic of Cancer and **Tropic of Capricorn** are imaginary lines at about 23°27" north and south of the equator, at the point where the sun changes its course over the earth's surface. Most deserts are found along these two lines. The area between the two lines is known as **the tropics**, and most rain forests are found in this region.

Tubers are short, thick parts of the underground stems of certain plants. They are covered in small bumps.

Tundra is the belt of land between the Arctic icecap and the treeline. Rough scrub is the only vegetation found in this region.

Understory is the name for the smaller trees and bushes that make up the middle level in a rain forest, below the tops of the taller trees.

Volcanoes are openings in the earth's crust from which hot, molten rock and gas may leak and cover the surrounding land.

Wildwoods are ancient woodlands in their natural state, inhabited by their original species.

Woodlands are areas of land in temperate countries, where many trees grow close together.

INDEX

NOTES

NOTES

NOTES

NOTES

NOTES